Mortimeriados by Michael Drayton

The Lamentable Civell Warres of Edward the Second and the Barrons.

Michael Drayton was born in 1563 at Hartshill, near Nuneaton, Warwickshire, England. The facts of his early life remain unknown.

Drayton first published, in 1590, a volume of spiritual poems; The Harmony of the Church. Ironically the Archbishop of Canterbury seized almost the entire edition and had it destroyed.

In 1593 he published Idea: The Shepherd's Garland, 9 pastorals celebrating his own love-sorrows under the poetic name of Rowland. This was later expanded to a 64 sonnet cycle.

With the publication of The Legend of Piers Gaveston, Matilda and Mortimeriados, later enlarged and re-published, in 1603, under the title of The Barons' Wars. His career began to gather interest and attention.

In 1596, The Legend of Robert, Duke of Normandy, another historical poem was published, followed in 1597 by England's Heroical Epistles, a series of historical studies, in imitation of those of Ovid. Written in the heroic couplet, they contain some of his finest writing.

Like other poets of his era, Drayton wrote for the theatre; but unlike Shakespeare, Jonson, or Samuel Daniel, he invested little of his art in the genre. Between 1597 and 1602, Drayton was a member of the stable of playwrights who worked for Philip Henslowe. Henslowe's Diary links Drayton's name with 23 plays from that period, and, for all but one unfinished work, in collaboration with others such as Thomas Dekker, Anthony Munday, and Henry Chettle. Only one play has survived; Part 1 of Sir John Oldcastle, which Drayton wrote with Munday, Robert Wilson, and Richard Hathwaye but little of Drayton can be seen in its pages.

By this time, as a poet, Drayton was well received and admired at the Court of Elizabeth 1st. If he hoped to continue that admiration with the accession of James 1st he thought wrong. In 1603, he addressed a poem of compliment to James I, but it was ridiculed, and his services rudely rejected.

In 1605 Drayton reprinted his most important works; the historical poems and the Idea. Also published was a fantastic satire called The Man in the Moon and, for the for the first time the famous Ballad of Agincourt.

Since 1598 he had worked on Poly-Olbion, a work to celebrate all the points of topographical or antiquarian interest in Great Britain. Eighteen books in total, the first were published in 1614 and the last in 1622.

In 1627 he published another of his miscellaneous volumes. In it Drayton printed The Battle of Agincourt (an historical poem but not to be confused with his ballad on the same subject), The Miseries of Queen Margaret, and the acclaimed Nimphidia, the Court of Faery, as well as several other important pieces.

Drayton last published in 1630 with The Muses' Elizium.

Michael Drayton died in London on December 23rd, 1631. He was buried in Westminster Abbey, in Poets' Corner. A monument was placed there with memorial lines attributed to Ben Jonson.

Index of Contents

To the Excellent and Most Accomplish'd Ladie, Lucie Countesse of Bedford.

Rrrest of Ladies, all, of all I have,
Anchor of my poore Tempest-beaten state,
Which givest life, to that life Nature gave,
And to thy selfe, doest onely consecrate:
My hopes true Goddesse, guider of my fate,
Vouchsafe to grace what here to light is brought,
Begot by thy sweet hand, borne of my thought.
And though I sing of this tumultuous rage,
Still paynting passions in these Tragedies,
Thy milder lookes, this furie can aswage,
Such is the vertue of thy sacred eyes,
Which doe contayne a thousand purities;
And lyke them selves, can make their obiect such,
As doth Th'elixar all things it doth tuch.
Sweet fruite, sprong from that ever sacred tree,
That happie wombe from whom thou lyfe do'st take,
And with that lyfe, gives vertue unto thee,
Thus made of her, her lyke of thee to make,
Shee lou'd for thee, thou honour'd for her sake;
And eithers good, from other so deriued,
Yet shee, nor thou, of any due depriued.
The Harringtons, whose house thy byrth hath blest,
Adding such honour to theyr familie,
And famous Bedfords greatnes still increast,
Raysing the height of theyr Nobilitie,
That Earledomes tytle more to dignifie?
That Vertue lyuely pictur'd forth in thee,
May truly be discernd, what shee should be.
And Lawrell-crowned Sidney, Natures pride,

Whom heaven to earth, but onely shew'd this good,
Betwixt the world, and thee did then devide,
His fame, and vertues, which both equall stood,
The world his fame, to thee of her owne blood
Hee gave his vertues, that in his owne kind,
His never-matched worth might be enshrin'd.
That whilst they boast but of their sun-burnt brayns,
Which Tramontani long have termd us so,
With all their Po's, their Tyburs, and their Rheyn's,
Greeuing to see how tidefull Thames shall flowe,
Our Groues which for the gracefull Muses growe:
Thy name shall be the glorie of the North,
The fayrest fruit that ever shee brought forth.
And in despight of tyranizing times,
This hope great Lady yet to thee is left,
Thy name shall lyue in steele-out-during rimes,
Still scorning ages sacraligious theft,
What fame doth keepe, can never be bereft:
Nor can thy past-priz'd honour ever die,
If lynes can gyue thee immortalitie.
Leauing unto succeeding times to see,
How much thy sacred gyfts I did adore.
What power thy vertues ever had in mee,
And what thou were compar'd with those before,
Which shall in age, thy youth againe restore:
And still shall ad more vigor to thy fame,
Then earthly honors, or a Countesse name.
Proclayming unto ages yet to come,
Whilst Bedford lyu'd, what lyuing Bedford was,
Enclosing thee in this immortall toombe,
More durable then letter-graven brasse,
To shewe what thy great power could bring to passe,
And other hopes I utterly refuse,
And thou my hope, my Lady, and my Muse.
Your Honors ever devoted servaunt
Michael Drayton.

To the Right Honorable Lady, Lucie Countesse of Bedford.

When God this wondrous Creature did create,
This ever-mouing body, this huge weight,
Whose head, whose lofty head high situate,
Is crown'd with starrs & constellations bright.
Hee causd the same one certaine way to moue,
Which moouing (some say) doth sweet tunes beget,
Another way the Sunne and Planets proue,

For they from thence moue where the sun doth set;
Yet he the Pole-star, Cynosura cleere,
Causd steddily to stand, though heaven did gyre,
For an example to mens actions heere:
Madam, you are the starre of his desire;
Whilst hee his thoughts heaven moves, ô gracious bee,
And wonders in your Creature you shall see.
Your honors and eternities Humble,
E. B.

Mortimeriados

The lowring heaven had mask'd her in a clowde,
Dropping sad teares upon the sullen earth,
Bemoning in her melancholly shrowde,
The angry starres which raign'd at Edwards birth,
With whose beginning ended all our mirth.
Edward the second, but the first of shame,
Scourge of the crowne, eclipse of Englands fame.

Whilst in our blood, ambition hotely boyles,
The Land bewailes her, like a wofull Mother,
On every side besieg'd with ciuill broyles,
Her deerest chyldren murthering one another,
Yet shee in silence forc'd her griefe to smother:
Groning with paine, in trauaile with her woes,
And in her torment, none to helpe her throwes.

What care would plot, discention striues to crosse,
Which like an earthquake rents the tottering state;
Abroade in warres we suffer publique losse,
At home, betrayd with grudge and priuate hate,
Faction attending blood-shed and debate;
Confusion thus our Countries peace confounds,
No helpe at hand, and mortall be her wounds.

Thou Church then swelling in thy mightines,
Thou which should'st be this poore sick bodyes soule,
O nurse not factions which should'st sinne suppresse,
And with thy members should'st all griefe condole,
Perswade thy hart and not thy head controle;
Humble thy selfe, dispence not with the word,
Take Peters keyes, but cast aside his sword.

The ragefull fire which burnt Carnaruans brest,
Blowne with revenge of Gauestons disgrace,

Awakes the Barrons from their nightly rest,
And maketh way to give the Spensers place,
Whose friendship Edward onely doth embrace;
By whose alurements he is fondly led,
To leave his Queene, and flie his lawful bed.

This Planet stirr'd up that tempestious blast
By which our fortunes Anchorage was torne,
The storme where-with our spring was first desac'd,
Whereby all hope unto the ground was borne:
Hence came the griefe, the teares, the cause to mourne.
This bred the blemish which her beauty staind,
Whose ugly scarr's, to after-times remaind.

In all this heat his greatnes first began,
The serious subject of my sadder vaine,
Great Mortimer, the wonder of a man,
Whose fortunes heere my Muse must entertaine,
And from the grave his griefes must yet complaine,
To shew our vice nor vertues never die,
Though under ground a thousand yeeres we lie.

Thys gust first threw him on that blessed Coast
Which never age discovered before:
This luckie chaunce drew all King Edward lost,
This shypwrack cast the prize upon his shore,
And thys all-drowning Deluge gave him more;
From hence the sunne of his good fortune shone,
The fatall step, to Edwards fatall throne.

That unckle now, whose name this Nephew bare,
The onely comfort of the wofull Queene,
And from his cradle held him as his care,
And still the hope of all his house had beene,
Whilst yet this deep hart-goring wound is greene,
On this well-seene aduantage wisely wrought,
To place him highly in her princely thought.

He saw his inclination from his birth,
A mighty spirit, a minde which did aspire;
Not of the drossy substance of the earth,
But of the purest element of fire,
Which sympathizing with his owne desire,
Name, nature, feature, all did so agree,
That still in him, himselfe he still might see.

The temper of his nobler moouing part,
Had that true tutch which purified his blood,

Insusing thoughts of honor in his hart,
Whose flaggie feathers were not soyld in mud,
The edge he bare declar'd the mettall good;
The towring pitch wherein he flew for fame,
Declar'd the ayrie whence the Eagle came.

Worthy the Grand-chyld of so great a sier,
Brave Mortimer who liu'd whilst Long-shanks raign'd,
Our second Arthur, whom all times admire,
At Kenelworth the Table round ordayn'd,
And therein Armes, a hundreth Knights maintaind;
A hundreth gallant Ladies in his Court,
Whose stately presence royaliz'd this sport.

And whilst this poore wife-widdowed Queene alone,
In thys dispayring passion pines away,
Beyond all hope, to all but heaven unknowne,
A little sparke which yet in secrete lay,
Breakes forth in flame, and turnes her night to day,
The wofull winter of her sorrowes cheering,
Even as the world at the faire Sunnes appearing.

Yet still perplexed in these hard extreames,
All meanes deprest which might her faith prefer,
Blacke foggs oppos'd in those cleere-shining beames,
Which else might lend their friendly light to her,
This in her lookes direfull revenge doth stir:
Which strange eclipse plac'd in this irefull signe,
Our Countries plague and ruine might diuine.

Her snowy curled brow makes anger smile,
Her laughing frowne gives beauty better grace,
Blushing disdaine, disdaine doth quite exile,
Sweet love and silence wrestling in her face,
Two capering Cupids in her eyes do chase;
Her veynes like tydes oft swelling with delight,
Making Vermilion faire, white more then white.

Her beauty florish'd whilst her fauours fade,
Her hopes growne old, but her desires be yong,
Her power wants power her passion to perswade,
Her sexe is weake, her will is over-strong,
Patience pleades pitty, but revenge her wrong;
What reason urgeth, rage doth still denie,
With arguments of wrathfull jealousie.

Pale Jealousie, child of insatiate love,
Of hart-sick thoughts with melancholie bred,

A hell tormenting feare no faith can moue,
By discontent with deadly poyson fed,
With heedlesse youth and error vainely led,
A mortall plague, a vertue-drowning flood,
A hellish fire, not quenched but with blood.

The hate-swolne Lords with furie set on fire,
Whom Edwards wrongs to vengeance doe prouoke,
With Lancaster and Herford now conspire,
No more to beare the Spensers seruile yoke,
The bonds of their alegiance they have broke:
Resolu'd with blood theyr libertie to buy,
To live with honor, or with fame to dye.

Amid thys faction Mortimer doth enter,
The gastly Prologue to thys tragick act:
His youth and courage boldly bids him venter,
And tells him still how strongly he was backt:
Synon perswades howe Illion might be sackt;
The people still applauding in his eares,
The fame and credite of the Mortimers.

Thys vapor-kindled Commet drew her eyes,
Which now began his streamie flagge to reare;
This beauty-blushing orient of his rise,
Her clowdy frownes doth with his brightnes cleare,
The joyfull'st sight that ever did appeare;
The messenger of light, her happy starre,
Which told her now the dawning was not farre.

As after pale-fac'd Night, the Morning fayre
The burning Lampe of heaven doth once erect,
With her sweet Crimson sanguining the ayre,
On every side with streakie dappl's fleckt,
The circled roofe in white and Azure deckt,
Such colour to her cheekes these newes do bring,
Which in her face doth make a second spring.

Yet trembling at the Spensers Lordly power,
Their wrongs, oppression, and controling pride,
Th'unconstant Barrons, wauering every houre,
The fierce encounter of this raging tyde,
No stratagem yet strongly policied;
Shee from suspition seemingly retyers,
Carelesse in shew of what she most desires.

Grounded aduice, in danger seldom trips,
The deadliest poyson, skill can safely drinke,

Fore-sight stands fast, where giddy rashnes slips,
Wisdome seemes blinde, when eyed as a Linxe
Prevention speaketh all but what he thinks;
The deadliest hate, with smyles securely stands,
Revenge in teares doth ever wash his hands.

Loe for her safetie this shee must desemble,
A benefite which women have by kind,
The neerest colour finely to resemble,
Suppressing thus the greatnes of her mind,
Now is shee shrowded closely under wind,
And at her prayers (poore soule) shee plainly ment,
A silly Queene, a harmelesse innocent.

The least suspition cunningly to heale,
Still in her lookes humilitie shee beares,
With patience she with mightines must deale,
So policie religions habite weares,
He's mad which takes a Lyon by the eares.
This knew the Queene, and this well know the wise,
This must they learne, which toyle in Monarchies.

Torlton the learnedst Prelate in the Land,
Upon a text of politicks to preach,
Car'd not on Paules preciser poynts to stand,
Poore Moralls to beleeuing men to teach,
For he at Kingdomes had a further reach:
This learned Tutor, Isabell had taught,
In nicer poynts then ever Edward sought.

Now in meane time, the smothered flame brake forth,
The Mortimers march from the westerne playne,
The Lords in armes at Pomfret in the North,
The King from London, comes with might and mayne,
Their factious followers in the streetes are slayne.
No other thing is to be hop'd upon,
But horrour, death, and desolation.

Like as Sabrina from the Ocean flancks,
Comes sweeping in along the tawny sands,
And with her billowes tilting on the bancks,
Rowles in her flood upon the westerne strands,
Stretching her watrie armes along the lands,
With such great furie doe these legions ryse,
Filling the shores with lamentable cryes.

Thus of three hands, they all set up theyr rest,
And at the stake their lives they franckly lay,

Hee's like to winne who cuts his dealing best,
And for a Kingdome at the least they play,
The fayr'st in show must carrie all away;
And though the King himselfe in sequence came,
He sawe the Queene lay right to make his game.

But Fortune masking in this straunge disguise,
Whose prodigie, whose monster he was borne,
Now in his lyfe her power, t'anotomize,
Ordayning him her darling and her scorne,
His Tragedie her triumph to adorne.
Shee straight begins to bandy him about,
At thousand ods before the set goes out.

As when we see the spring-begetting Sunne,
In heavens black night-gowne covered from our sight,
And when he yet, but fewe degrees hath runne,
Some fennie fogge damps up his gladsome light,
That at his noon-sted he may shine more bright.
His cheerefull morning Fortune cloudeth thus,
To make his day more fayre, more glorious.

Edward whom daunger warnd to dread the worst,
Unto the hart with poysned ranckor stung,
Now for his crowne must scuffle if he durst,
Or else his scepter in the dust were flung,
To stop the head from which these mischiefes sprung.
First with the Marchers thinks it fit to cope,
On whom he knew lay all the Barrons hope.

Like to a whirle-wind comes this irefull King,
Whose presence soone the Welchmens power had staid,
The Cornish yet theyr forces fayld to bring,
And Lancaster too slacke forslow'd theyr ayd,
Faynt-harted friends, their succours long delayd.
Depriu'd of meanes, forlorne of farther good,
And wanting strength to stem so great a flood.

They who perceiu'd, their trust was thus betrayd,
Their long expected purpose thus to quayle,
How mischiefe still upon their fortune playd,
That they perforce their high-borne top must vayle,
This storme still blew so stifly on their sayle.
Of Edwards mercy now the depth must sound,
Where yet their Ankor might take hold on ground.

This tooke the King in presage of his good,
Who this event to his successe apply'd,

Which coold the furie of his boyling blood,
Before their force in armes he yet had try'd,
His sterne approch this easely molified
That on submission he dismist theyr power,
And sends them both as prisoners to the Tower.

Not cowardize but wisedome warnes to yield,
When Fortune aydes the proud insulting foe,
Before dishonour ever blot the field;
Where by aduantage hopes agayne may growe,
When as too weake to beare so great a blowe:
That whilst his pittie pardons them to live,
To his owne wrongs he full revenge might give.

Loe now my Muse must sing of dreadfull Arme,
And taske her selfe to tell of ciuill warres,
Of Ambuscados, stratagems, alarmes,
Of murther, slaughter, monstrous Massacarres,
Of blood, of wounds, of never-healed scarres,
Of battailes fought by brother against brother,
The Sonne and Father one against the other.

O thou great Lady, Mistris of my Muse,
Renowned Lucie, vertues truest frend,
Which doest a spyrit into my spyrit infuse,
And from thy beames the light I have dost lend,
Into my verse thy lyuing power extend.
O breathe new lyfe to write this Tragicke storie,
Assist me now brave Bedford for thy glorie.

Whilst in the Tower the Mortimers are mew'd,
The Barrons drew their forces to a head,
Whom Edward (spurd with vengeance) still pursu'd
By Lancaster and famous Herford led,
Toward eithers force, forth-with both Armies sped.
At Burton both in camping for the day,
Where they must trye who beares the spurres away.

Upon the East from bushie Needwoods side,
There riseth up an easie clyming hill,
At whose fayre foote the siluer Trent doth slide,
And all the shores with ratling murmure ill,
Whose tumbling waues the flowrie Meadowes swill,
Upon whose streame a Bridge of wondrous strength,
Doth stretch her selfe, neere fortie Arches length.

Upon this mount the King his Tents hath fixt,
And in the Towne the Barrons lye in sight,

This famous Ryuer risen so betwixt,
Whose furie yet prolong'd this deadly fight,
The passage stopp'd, not to be wonne by might.
Things which presage both good and ill there bee,
Which heaven fore-shewes, yet will not let us see.

The raging flood hath drownd up all her foards,
Sok'd in excesse of cloud-congealed teares,
And steepes the bancks within her watrie hoards,
Supping the whir-pooles from the quaggie mears,
Now doth shee washe her tressed rushie hayrs.
Swolne with the dropsie in her grieued woombe,
That this her channell must become a Toombe.

O warlike Nation hold thy conquering hand,
Even sencelesse things doe warne thee yet to pawse,
Thy Mother soyle on whom thy feete doe stand,
O then infrindge not Natures sacred lawes,
Still runne not headlong into mischiefes iawes:
Yet stay thy foote in murthers ugly gate,
Ill comes too soone, repentance ost too late.

And can the cloudes weepe over thy decay,
Yet not one drop fall from thy droughtie eyes?
Seest thou the snare yet wilt not shunne the way,
Nor yet be warn'd, by passed miseries?
Or ere too late, yet learne once to be wise.
A mischiefe seene, may easely be prevented,
But beeing hap'd, not help'd, yet still lamented.

Behold the Eagles, Lyons, Talbots, Bears,
The Badges of your famous ancestries,
And shall they now by their inglorious heyrs:
Be thus displayd against their families?
Reliques unworthie of theyr progenies.
Those Beastes you beare doe in their kinds agree
And then those Beasts more sauage will you bee?

Cannot the Scot of your late slaughter boast?
And are you yet scarce healed of the sore?
Is't not inough you have already lost,
But your owne madnes now must make it more?
Your Wiues and Children pittied you before.
But when your own blood, your own swords imbrue,
Who pitties them, which once have pittied you?

What, shall the Sister weepe her Brothers death,
Who sent her Husband to his timelesse grave?

The Nephewe moane his Unckles losse of breath,
Which did his Father of his lyfe depraue?
Who shall have mind your memories to saue?
Or shall he buriall to his friend afford,
Who lately put his Sonne unto the sword?

But whilst the King, and Lords in counsell sit,
Yet in conclusion variably doe hover,
See how misfortune still her time can fit:
Such as were sent the Country to discover,
Have found a way to land their forces over.
Ill newes hath wings, and with the winde doth goe,
Comfort's a Cripple, and comes ever slow.

And Edward fearing Lancasters supplyes,
Great Surry, Richmond, and his Pembrooke sent,
On whose successe his chiefest hope relyes,
Under whose conduct halfe his Armie went,
And he himselfe, and Edmond Earle of Kent,
Upon the hill in sight of Burton lay.
Watching to take aduantage of the day.

Stay Surry stay, thou maist too soone begon;
Stay till this rage be some-what over-past,
Why runn'st thou thus to thy destruction?
Pembrooke and Richmond, whether doe you hast?
Never seeke sorrow, for it comes too fast.
Why striue you thus to passe this fatall flood,
To fetch new wounds, and shed your neerest blood?

Great Lancaster, sheath up thy conquering sword,
On Edwards Armes, whose edge thou should'st not whet,
Thy naturall Nephew, and thy soveraigne Lord,
Both one, one blood, and both Plantaginet.
Canst thou thy oth to Longshanks thus forget?
Yet call to minde, before all other things,
Our vowes must be perform'd to Gods and Kings.

Knowe, noble Lord, it better is to end,
Then to proceed in things rashly begun:
Which out ill counseld worser doe offend,
Speech hath obtain, where weapons have not won;
By good perswasion what cannot be done?
And when all other hopes and helps be past,
Then fall to Armes, but let that be the last.

The winds are husht, no little breth doth blow,
The calmed ayre as all amazed stood,

The earth with roring trembleth below,
The Sunne besmear'd his glorious face in blood,
The fearfull Heards bellowing as they were wood:
The Drums and Trumpets give a signall sound,
With such a noyse as they had torne the ground.

The Earles now charging with three hundred horse,
The Kings vantgard assay the Bridge to win,
Forcing the Barrons to devide their force,
T'auoyde the present danger they were in:
Never till now the horror doth begin;
That if th'elements our succour had not sought,
All had that day beene to confusion brought.

Now frō the hill the Kings maine power comes downe,
Which had Aquarius to their valiant guide,
Brave Lancaster and Herford from the towne,
Doe issue forth upon the other side:
The one assailes, the other munified.
Englands Red crosse upon both sides doth flye,
Saint George the King, Saint George the Barrons cry.

Even as a bustling tempests rouzing blasts,
Upon a Forrest of old-branched Oakes,
Downe upon heapes their climing bodies casts,
And with his furie teyrs their mossy loaks,
The neighbour groues resounding with the stroaks,
With such a clamor and confused woe,
To get the Bridge these desperate Armies goe.

Now must our famous and victorious bowes,
With which our Nation Kingdoms did subdue,
First send their darting arrowes against those
Whose sinewed armes against their foes them drew;
These winged weapons, mourning as they flew,
Cleave to the strings, with very terror slack,
As to the Archers they would faine turne back.

The battered Caskes, with Battel-Axes strokes,
Besnow the soyle with drifts of scattered plumes,
The trampling presse stirre up such duskie smokes
Which choke the ayre with reekie smothering fumes,
Which rising up, into a clowde consumes;
As though the heaven had muffled her in black,
Lothing to see this lamentable sack.

Behold the remnant of Troyes famous stocke,
Laying on blowes as Smithes on Anuiles strike,

Grappling together in this fearfull shock,
The like presse forth, t'incounter with the like,
And then reculing to the push of pyke:
Yet not a foote doth eyther give to eyther,
Now one the ods, then both alike, then neither.

Even as you see a field of standing Corne,
When in faire lune some easie gale doth blow,
How up and downe the spyring eares are borne,
And with the blasts like Billowes come and goe,
As golden streamers wauing to and fro,
Thus on the suddaine runne they on amaine,
Then straight by force are driuen backe againe.

Heer lyes a heap, halfe slaine, halfe chok'd, halfe drownd,
Gasping for breth amongst the slymie seggs,
And there a sort falne in a deadly swound,
Scrawling in blood upon the muddy dreggs:
Heere in the streame, swim bowels, armes and leggs
One kills his foe, his braine another cuts,
Ones feet intangled in anothers guts.

One his owne hands in his owne blood defiles,
Another from the Bridges height doth fall,
Some dash'd to death upon the stony pyles,
Some in theyr gore upon the pauement sprall,
The carkasses lye heaped like a wall:
Such hideous shreeks the bedlam Souldiers breath,
As though the Spirits had howled from beneath.

The mangled bodies diuing in the streame,
Now up, now downe, like tumbling Porpose swim,
The water cover'd with a bloody creame,
To the beholder horrible and grim:
Heere lies a head, and there doth lye a lym;
Which in the sands the swelling waters souse,
That all the shores seeme like a slaughter-house.

It seem'd the very wounds for griefe did weepe,
To feele the temper of the slicing blade,
The sencelesse steele in blood it selfe did steepe,
To see the wounds his sharpe-ground edge had made,
Whilst kinsman, kinsman, friend, doth friend invade,
Such is the horror of these ciuill broyles,
When with our blood, we fat our natiue soyles.

This faction still defying Edwards might,
Edmond of Woodstock, famous Earle of Kent,

Charging the foe againe renewes the fight,
Upon the Barrons forces almost spent,
Who now againe supplying succours sent.
And now a second conflict doth begin,
The English Lords like Tygars flying in.

Like as an exhalation hote and dry,
Amongst the ayre-bred moyftie vapors throwne,
Spetteth his lightning forth outragiously,
Renting the thick clowdes with a thunder-stone,
As though the huge all-covering heaven did grone,
Such is the garboyle of this conflict then,
Brave Englishmen, encountring Englishmen.

Even as proude Pyrrhùs entring Iltion,
Couragious Talbot with his shield him bare,
Clifford and Moubray, seconding anon,
Audley and Gifford thrunging for their share,
Elmbridge and Balsmer in the thickest are:
Pell-mell together flyes this furious power,
Like to the falling of some mighty Tower.

Mountfort and Teis, your worths faine would I speake,
But that your valure can but ill deserue,
Brave Denuile, heere I from thy prayse must breake,
And from thy prayses Willington must swarue,
Great Damory, heere must thy glory starue;
Concealing many, most deseruing blame,
Because their acts doe quench my sacred flame.

O that those Armes in conquests had been borne,
And that, that battered fame-engraven shield,
Should in those ciuill massacres be torne
Which bare the marks of many a bloody field:
O that our armes had power their Armes to weeld.
That since that time, the stones for very dreed,
Against foule stormes could teary moisture sheed.

O had you shap'd your valures first by them
Who summon'd Akon with an English drum,
Or marched on to faire Ierusalem,
T'inlarge the bounds of famous Christendome,
Or with Christs warriors slept about his toombe,
Then ages had immortaliz'd your fame,
Where now my song can be but of your shame.

Death following on, feare ever in their eyes,
Grieued with wounds, the conquered Barrons fled,

And now the King enrich'd with victories,
Hath in the field his glorious Ensignes spred,
This in his thoughts againe fresh courage bred,
And somwhat drawes th'unconstant peoples harts,
Who equall peyz'd, yet way'd to neither parts.

And wanting ground, they unresolued are,
King Edwards friends, agaynst the rebels cry,
The Barrons plead their Countries onely care,
Exclayming on the Princes tyrannie,
Hee vrg'd obedience, they their libertie.
Both under colour, carefull of the state,
Hee right, and they their wrongs expostulate.

Some fewe them selves in Sanctuaries hide,
In mercie of the priuiledged place,
Yet are their bodyes so unsanctifide,
As scarce their soules can ever hope for grace,
A poore dead lyfe, this draweth out a space.
Hate stands without, and horror sits within,
Prolonging shame, yet pard'ning not their sinne.

At fatall Pomfret gathering head at length,
When they of all extreamities had tasted,
Where yet before they could recover strength,
King Edward followeth whilst his fortune lasted,
Unto whose ayde the Earle of Carlell hasted.
With troupes of bow-men and ranck-riding bands,
Of Westmer, Cumber, and Northumberlands.

Mad and amaz'd, nor knowing what to doe,
Surpriz'd by this late mischieuous event,
Seeing at hand their utter overthrowe,
And in despight how crossely all things went,
Fortune her selfe to their destruction bent;
In all disorder head-long on they runne,
To end with blood, what was with blood begunne.

Lyke as a heard of silly hartlesse Deare,
Whom hote-spurd Huntsmen fiercely doe pursue,
In brakes and bushes falling heere and there,
Yet when no way the hounds they can eschew,
Now flying back from whence of late they flew,
Hem'd on each side with hornes rechating blast,
Head-long them selves into the toyles doe cast.

To Borough bridge by fate appoynted thus,
Where lyke false Raynard, falser Herckley lay,

Bridges to Barrons ever ominous,
There to renewe this latest deadly fray,
O heere begins the blackest dismall day,
The birth of horror, hower of wrath that yet,
The very soyle seemes to remember it.

Heere is not Death contented with the dead,
Nor vengeance is with vengeance satisfied,
Blood-shed by blood-shed still is nourished,
And mischiefe meanes no more her store to hide,
Strange sorts of torments heaven doth now prouide,
That dead men should in miserie remayne,
And in lyuing death should dye with payne.

Thus rules the world, a world why sawe I so,
Worst is the world, yet worser must I name it,
Nights vgli'st night, hells bitter'st hell of woe,
So ill as slaunder never can defame it,
That shame her selfe is sham'd, seeking to shame it,
Could envie speake, what envie can expresse,
In saying most, that most should make it lesse.

Heere noble Herford, Bohun breathes his last,
Crowne of true Knight-hood, flower of Chiualrie,
But Lancaster their torment lives to tast,
Who perrish now with endlesse obloquie,
O vanquisht conquest, loosing victorie,
That where the sword for pittie leaves to spill,
There extreame justice should begin to kill.

O subject for some tragick Muse to sing,
Of fiue great Earledomes at one time possest,
Sonne, Unckle, Brother, Grandchild to a King,
With fauours, friends, and earthly honours blest,
But see on earth, heere is no place of rest.
These Fortunes gyfts, and she to shew her power,
Takes lyfe, and these, and all within an hower.

The wretched Mother tearing of her hayre,
Bewayles the time this fatall warre begunne,
Lyke grave-borne gosts, amaz'd and mad with feare,
To view the quartered carkasse of her Sonne,
With hideous shreeks through streetes & wayes doth runne.
And seeing none to help, none heare her crye,
Some drownd, some stabd, some starud, some strangled die.

Lyke gastly death the aged Father stands,
Weeping his Sonne, bemoning of his wife,

Shee murthered by her owne blood-guiltie hands,
Hee flaughtered by the executioners knife,
Sadly sits downe to ende his hatefull life;
Banning the earth, and cursing at the ayre
Upon his poyniard falleth in dispayre.

The wofull widdowe for her Lord distrest,
Whose breathlesse body cold death doth benum,
Her little Infant leaning on her breast,
Rings in her eares, when will my Father come?
Doth wish that she were deafe, or it were dombe.
Clipping each other, weeping both togeather,
Shee for her Lord, the poore babe for his Father.

The ayre is poysned with the dampie stinck,
Which most contagious pestilence doth breed,
The glutted earth her fill of gore doth drinck,
Which from unburied bodies doth proceede,
Rauens and dogs on dead men onely feede;
In every Coast thus doe our eyes behold,
Our sinnes by judgement of the heavens controld.

Lyke as a Wolfe returning from the foyle,
Hauing full stuft his flesh-engorged panch,
Tumbles him downe to wallowe in the soyle,
With cooling breath his boyling mawe to stanch,
Scarce able now to mooue his lustlesse hanch.
Thus after slaughter Edward breathlesse stood,
As though his sword had surfeted with blood.

Heere endeth life, yet heere death cannot end,
And heere begins, what Edwards woes begun,
Nor his pretence, falls as he doth pretend,
Nor hath he wone, what he by battell wone,
All is not done, though almost all undone,
Whilst power hath raign'd still policie did lurke,
Seldome doth mallice want a meane to worke.

The King now by the conquering Lords consent,
Who by this happie victorie grew strong,
Summons at Yorke a present Parliament,
To plant his right, and helpe the Spensers wrong,
From whence agayne his minions greatnes sprung,
Whose counsell still, in all their actions crost,
Th'inraged Queene whom all misfortunes tost.

But miseries which seldome come alone,
Thicke in the necks one of another fell,

Meane while the Scots heere make invasion,
And Charles of France doth thence our powers expell,
The grieued Commons more and more rebell.
Mischiefe on mischiefe, curse doth followe curse,
Plague after plague, and worse ensueth worse.

For Mortimer this wind yet rightly blewe,
Darckning their eyes which else perhaps might see,
Whilst Isabell who all aduantage knewe,
Is closely plotting his deliverie,
Now fitly drawne by Torltons policie:
Thus by a Queene, a Bishop, and a Knight,
To check a King, in spight of all dispight.

A drowsie potion shee by skill hath made,
Whose secret working had such wonderous power,
As could the sence with heauie sleepe invade,
And mortifie the patient in one hower,
As though pale death the body did devower;
Nor for two dayes might opened be his eyes,
By all meanes Arte or Phisicke could devise.

Thus sits this great Enchauntresse in her Cell,
Inuironed with spyrit-commaunding charmes,
Her body censed with most sacred smell,
With holy fiers her liquors now shee warmes,
Then her with sorcering instruments she armes.
And from her hearbs the powerfull iuyce she wrong,
To make the poyson forcible and strong.

Reason might judge, doubts better might aduise,
And as a woman, feare her hand have stayd,
Waying the strangenesse of the interprize,
The daunger well might have her sex dismayd,
Fortune, distrust, suspect, to be betrayd;
But when they leave of vertue to esteeme,
They greatly erre which thinke them as they seeme.

Their plighted fayth, when as they list they leave,
Their love is cold, their lust, hote, hote their hate,
With smiles and teares these Serpents doe deceaue,
In their desires they be insatiate,
Their will no bound, and their revenge no date.
All feare exempt, where they at ruine ayme,
Covering their sinne with their discovered shame.

Medea pittifull in tender yeares,
Untill with Iason she would take her flight,

Then mercilesse her Brothers lymmes she teares,
Betrayes her Father, flyes away by night,
Nor Nations, Seas, nor daungers could affright;
Who dyed with heate, nor could abide the wind,
Now like a Tigar falls unto her kind.

Now waits the Queene fitt'st time, as might behoue,
Their ghostly Father for their speed must pray,
Their seruants seale these secrets up with love,
Their friends must be the meane, the guide, the way,
And he resolue on whom the burthen lay;
This is the summe, the all, if this neglected,
Never againe were meane to be expected.

Thus, while hee liv'd a prysoner in the Towre,
The Keepers oft with feasts he entertaind,
Which as a stale, serves fitly at this howre,
The tempting bayte wher-with his hookes were traind,
The lavish banquet now he had ordaind,
And after cates when they their thirst should quench,
He sawc'd their wine with thys approoved drench.

And thus become the keeper of the kayes,
In steele-bound locks he safely lodg'd the Guard:
Then lurking forth by the most secret wayes,
Not now to learne his compasse by the Card,
With corded ladders which hee had prepard,
Now up these proude aspyring walls doth goe,
Which seeme to scorne they should be mastred so.

They soundly sleepe, now must his wits awake,
A second Theseus through a hells extreames,
The sonne of loue, new toyles must undertake,
Of walls, of gates, of watches, woods, and streame.
And let them tell King Edward of their dreames:
For ere they wak'd out of this brainsick traunce,
He hopes to tell thys noble iest in Fraunce.

The sullen night in mistie rugge is wrapp'd,
Powting the day had tarryed up so long,
The Evening in her darksome dungion clapp'd,
And in that place the swarty clowdes were hong,
Downe from the West the half-fac'd Cynthia flong
As shee had posted forth to tell the Sonne,
What in his absence in her Court was done.

The glymmering starr's like Sentinels in warre,
Behind the Clowdes as thieves doe stand to pry,

And through false loope-holes looking out a farre,
To see him skirmish with his destenie,
As they had held a counsell in the Sky,
And had before consulted with the night,
Shee should be darke, and they would hide their light.

In deadly silence all the shores are hush'd,
Onely the Shreechowle sounds to the assault,
And Isis with a troubled murmure rush'd,
As shee had done her best to hide the fault,
A little whispering moov'd within the vault,
Made with his tuching softly as he went,
Which seem'd to say it furthered his intent.

This wondrous Queene, whom care from rest had kept,
Now for his speed to heaven holds up her hands,
A thousand thoughts within her bosome heap'd,
Now in her Closset listning still she stands,
And though devided as in sundry strands,
Yet absent, present in desires they bee,
For minds discerne, where eyes could never see.

Loe now he thinks he vaulteth in her sight,
Still taking courage, strengthned by her words,
Imagining shee sported with delight,
To see his strong armes stretch the tackling coards,
And oft a smyle unto his toyle affords:
And when shee doubted danger, might her heare,
Call him her soule, her life, her Mortimer.

Nowe doth shee wooe the walls, intreat and kisse,
And then protests to memorize the place,
And to adorne it with a Piramis,
Whose glory wrack of time should not deface.
Then to the cord shee turnes her selfe a space,
And promiseth, if that should set him free,
A sacred relique it should ever bee.

Shee saith, the small clowds issuing from his breath,
Seasond with sweet from whence they lately came,
Should cleere the ayre from pestilence and death,
And like Promethian life-begetting flame,
Pure bodies in the element should frame;
And to what part of heaven they hapt to stray,
There should they make another milkie way.

Attain the top his tyred lymm's to breath,
Mounted in tryumph on his miseries,

The gentle earth salutes him from beneath:
And cover'd with the comfortable skyes,
Lightned with beames of Isabella's eyes,
Downe from the Turret desperatly doth slide;
Now for a kingdome, Fortune be his guide.

As hee descends, so doe her eyes ascend,
As feare had fixt them to behold his fall;
Then from the sight, away her sight doth bend,
When chilly coldnes doth her hart appall,
Then out for helpe shee suddainly doth call;
Silent againe, watching if ought should hap,
Her selfe might be the ground, his grave her lap.

Now doth she court the gentle calmie ayre,
And then againe shee doth coniure the winde;
Now doth she try to stop the night by prayer,
And then with spells the heauy sence to binde;
Then by the burning Tapers shee divinde;
Now shee intreats faire Thames that hee might passe
The Hellespont where her Leander was.

The brushing murmure stills her like a song,
Yet fearing least the streame should fall in love,
Envies the drops which on his tresses hong,
Imagining the waues to stay him strove;
And when the billowes with his brest he droue,
Grieued there-with, shee turnes away her face,
Jealous least hee the billowes should embrace.

Shee likneth him to the transformed Bull,
Which curll'd the fayre flood with his Iuory flanck,
When on his backe he bare the lovely trull,
Floting along unto the Cretan banck,
Comparing this to that lasciuious pranck,
And swears then hee, no other loue there were,
If shee Europa had been present there.

Thus seekes he life, encourag'd by his love,
Yet for his love his life he doth eschue,
Danger in him a deadly feare doth moue,
And feare envits him danger to pursue,
Rage stirr's revenge, revenge doth rage renve:
Danger and feare, rage and revenge at strife,
Life warr's with love, and love contends with life.

Thys angry Lyon hauing slypp'd his chayne,
Now like a Quartain, makes King Edward quake,

Who knew too well, ere he was caught againe,
Some of his flock his bloody thirst must slake;
And unawares intangled in this brake,
Sawe further vengeance hanging in the wind,
Knowing too well, the greatnes of his mind.

Thys once againe the world begins to worke,
Theyr hopes (at length) unto thys issue brought,
Whilst yet the Serpent in his Den doth lurke,
Of whom God knowes, the King full little thought,
The instrument which these devises wrought.
For ther's no treason woundeth halfe so deepe,
As that which doth in Princes bosoms sleepe.

Now must the Cleargie serue them for a cloke,
The Queene her state unto the time must fit,
But tis the Church-man which must strike the stroke,
Now must thys Prelate shew a statesmans wit,
They cast the plot, and March must manage it;
They both at home together lay on load,
And he the Agent to effect abroad.

Who sweetly tunes his well-perswading tong,
In pleasing musick to the French-kings ears,
The sad discourse of Isabellas wrong,
With tragick action forcing silent tears,
Moouing to pitty every one that hears,
That by discovery of thys foule reproch,
Old mischiefes so, might new be set abroch.

Whilst they are tempring in these home-bred iarres,
How for the Scot fit passage might be made,
To lay the ground of these succesfull warrs,
That hope might give him courage to invade,
And from the King the Commons to perswade;
That whilst at home his peace he would assure,
His further plague in Fraunce he might procure.

By these reports, all circumstances knowne,
Sounds Charles of Fraunce into the lists againe,
To ceaze on Guyen by Armes to clayme his owne,
Which Edward doth unlawfully detaine,
Homage for Pontieu, and for Aquitaine,
Revoking this dishonorable truce,
Vrg'd by his wrongs, and Isabels abuse.

The spirits thus rayz'd which haunt him day and night,
And on his fortune heaven doth ever lower,

Danger at hand, and mischiefe still in sight,
Ciuill sedition weakning still his power,
No ease of paine one minute in the hower:
T' intreat of peace with Charles, he now must send,
Else all his hopes in Fraunce were at an end.

Heere is the poynt wherein all poynts must end,
Which must be handled with no meane regard,
The prop whereon this building must depend,
Which must by leuell curiouslie be squard,
The cunningst descant that had yet beene hard.
Heere close conueyance must a meane prouide,
Else might the ambush easely be discride.

Or this must helpe, or nothing serues the turne,
This way, or no way, all must come about,
To blowe the fier which now began to burne,
Or tind the strawe before the brand went out,
This is the lot which must resolue the doubt,
To walke the path where Edward bears the light,
And take their ayme by leuell of his sight.

This must a counsell seriously debate,
In gravest judgements fit to be discust,
Beeing a thing so much consernes the state,
Edward in this, must to their wisedomes trust,
No whit suspecting but that all were just.
Especially the Church whose mouth shoud be,
The Oracle of truth and equitie.

Torlton whose tongue, mens eares in chaines could tye,
Whose words, even like a thunderbolt could pearce,
And were alowd of more aucthoritie,
Then was the Sibills olde diuining verse,
Which were of force a judgement to reverse:
Now for the Queene, with all his power doth stand,
To lay this charge on her well-guiding hand.

What helpes her presence to the cause might bring,
First as a wife, a sister, and a mother,
A Queene to deale, betwixt a King, and King,
To right her sonne, her husband, and her brother,
And each to her indifferent as the other:
Which colour serues to worke in these extreames,
That which (God knowes) King Edward never dreames.

Torlton is this thy spirituall pretence?
Would God thy thoughts were more spirituall,

Or lesse perswasiue were thy eloquence,
But ô thy actions are too temporall,
Thy reasons subtill and sophisticall:
Would all were true thy suposition sayth,
Thy arguments lesse force, or thou more fayth.

Thus is the matter managed with skill,
To his desires, their meanes thus to devise,
To thrust him on, to drawe them up the hill,
That by his strength, they might get power to rise,
This great Archmaster of all policies:
In the beginning wisely had forcast,
How ere things went, which way they must at last.

With sweetest hony, thus he baytes the snare,
And clawes the beast till he be in the yoke,
In golden cups he poyson doth prepare,
And tickles where he meanes to strike the stroke,
Giuing the bone whereas he meant to choke:
And by all helpes of Arte doth smooth the way,
To send his foe, downe head-long to decay.

Shee which thus fitly had both winde and tide,
And sawe her passage serue the hower so right,
Whilst things thus fadge are quicke dispatch applide,
To take her time whilst yet the day is light,
Who hath beene tyerd in trauell feares the night:
And finding all too much to change inclind,
And every toy soone altering Edwards mind.

Her followers such as frendlesse else had stood,
Supprest and troden with the Spensers pride,
Whose howses Edward branded had with blood,
And but with blood could not be satisfi'd,
Who for revenge did but the hower abide;
And knew all helpes, that mischiefe could inuent,
To shake the state, and further her intent.

Thus on the wronged, she her wrongs doth rest,
And unto poyson, poyson doth applie,
Her selfe oprest, to harden the oprest,
And with a spye, to intercept a spye,
An Enemie, against an Enemie.
Hee that will gaine what policie doth heede,
By Mercurie must deale, or never speede.

Now Mortimer, whose mayne was fully set,
Seeing by fortune all his hopes were crost,

His strugling still how he againe might get,
That which before his disaduantage lost,
Not once dismayd though in these tempests tost:
Nor in affliction is he overthrowne,
To Mortimer all Countries are his owne.

Englands an Ile where all his youth he spent,
Environ'd valure in it selfe is drownd,
But now he lives within the continent,
Which being boundlesse, honour hath no bound,
Here through the world, doth endlesse glory sound:
To fames rich treasure Time unlocks the dore,
Which angry Fortune had shut up before.

What wayes he of his wealth, our Wigmore left,
Let builded heapes, let Rocks and Mountaines stand,
Goods oft be held by wrong, first got by theft,
Birds have the ayre, Fish water, Men the land,
Alcides pitch'd his pillers in the sand.
Men looke up to the starres thereby to knowe,
As they doe progresse heaven, he earth should doe.

And to this end, did Nature part the ground,
Else had not man beene King upon the Sea,
Nor in depths her secrets had beene found,
If to all parts on firme had layne his way,
But she to shewe him where her wonders lay:
To passe the floods, this meane for him inuents,
To trample on these baser elements.

Never sawe France, no never till this day,
A mind more great, more free, more resolute,
Let all our Edwards say, what Edwards may,
Our Henries, Talbot, or our Mountacute,
To whom our royall conquests we impute:
That Charles him selfe, oft to the Peers hath sworne,
This man alone, the Destinies did scorne.

Vertue can beare, what can on Vertue fall,
Who cheapeneth honour, must not stand on price,
Who beareth heaven (they say) can well beare all,
A yeelding mind doth argue cowardize,
Our haps doe turne as chaunces on the dice.
Nor never let him from his hope remoue,
That under him hath mould, the starres aboue.

Let dull-braynd slaves contend for mud and earth,
Let blocks and stones, sweat but for blocks and stones,

Let peasants speake of plenty and of dearth,
Fame never lookes so lowe as on these drones,
Let courage manage Empiers, sit on thrones.
And he that Fortune at commaund will keepe,
He must be suer, he never let her sleepe.

Who wins her grace, must with atchiuements wooe her,
As shee is blind, so never had shee eares,
Nor must with puling eloquence goe to her,
Shee understands not sighes, she heares not prayers,
Flatterd shee flyes, controld shee ever feares;
And though a while shee nicely doe forsake it,
Shee is a woman, and at length will take it.

Nor never let him dreame once of a Crowne,
For one bad cast, that will give up his game,
And though by ill hap he be overthrowne,
Yet let him manage her, till shee be tame,
The path is set with danger leads to fame:
When Minos did the Graecians flight denie,
He made him wings, and mounted through the skie.

The cheerefull morning cleeres her cloudie browes,
The vaporie mists are all disperst and spred,
Now sleepie Time his lazie lims doth rouze,
And once beginneth to hold up his head,
Hope bloometh faire, whose roote was wel nere dead,
The clue of sorrowe to the end is ronne,
The bowe appeares to tell the flood is donne.

Nature lookes backe to see her owne decay,
Commaunding age to slacke her speedy pace,
Occasion forth her golden loake doth lay,
Whilst sorrowe paynts her wrinckle-withered face,
Day lengthneth day, and joyes doe joyes imbrace.
Now is she comming yet till she be heere,
My pen runnes slowe, each comma seemes a yeere.

She's now imbarck'd, slide billowes for her sake,
Whose eyes can make your aged Neptune yong,
Sweet Syrens from the chaulkie cleeus awake,
Rauish her eares with some inchaunting song,
Daunce the Lauoltos all the sands along:
It is not Venus on your floods doth passe,
But one more fayre then ever Venus was.

You scalie Dolphins gaze upon her eyes,
And never after with your kind make warre,

O steale the Musicke from her lips that flyes,
Whose accents like the tunes of Angels are,
Compard with whom Arions did but iarre.
Hugge them sweet ayre, and when the Seas doe rage,
Use them as charmes thy tempests to aswage.

Sweet Sea-nymphs flock in sholes upon the shores,
Fraunce kisse those feete whose steps thou first didst guide,
Present thy Queene with all thy gorgious store,
Now mayst thou revell in thy greatest pride:
Shyp mount to heaven, and be thou stellified,
And next that starr-fix'd Argosie alone,
There take thou up thy constellation.

Th' exceeding joy conceued by the Queene,
Or his content, to them I leave to gesse
Who but the subject of their thoughts have seene,
Who I am sure, if they the truth confesse,
Will say that silence onely can expresse:
And when with honor shee fit time could take,
With sweet embraces thus shee him bespake.

O Mortimer, great Mortimer quoth shee,
What angry power such mischiefe could devise,
To separate thy deerest Queene and thee,
Whom loves eternall union strongly tyes?
But seeing thee, unto my longing eyes
(Though guiltlesse they,) this penance is assignd,
To gaze upon thee untill they be blind.

Sweet face, quoth shee, how art thou changed thus,
Since beauty on this lovely front thou bor'st,
Like the yong Hunter fresh Hipolitus,
When in these curles my fauors first thou wor'st?
Now like great loue thy Iuno thou ador'st;
The Muses leave theyr double-topped throne,
And on thy temples make theyr Helicon.

Come tell mee now what griefe and danger is,
Of paine and pleasure in imprisonment,
At every breath the poynt shal be a kisse,
Which can restore consuming languishment,
A cordiall to comfort banishment;
And thou shalt find, that pleasures long restraind,
Be farre more pleasant when they once be gaind.

Now sweeten all thy sorrowes with delight,
Teach man-hood courtshyp, turne these broyles to love,

The day's nere ill that hast a pleasing night,
Ther's other warrs in hand, which thou must proue,
Warrs which no blood shall shed, nor sorrow moue:
And that sweet foe of whom thou winn'st the day,
Shall crowne thy tresses with tryumphant Bay.

And sith that tyme our better ease assures,
Let solace sit and rock thee on her brest,
And let thy sences say like Epicures,
Lets eate and drinke, and lay us downe to rest,
Like belly-Gods, to surfet at the feast;
Our day is cleere, then never doubt a shower,
Prince Edward is my sonne, England my dower.

Possessing this inestimable Iem,
What is there wanting to maintaine thy port?
Thy royall Mistresse wears a Diadem,
Thy high-pitchd pyneons sore beyond report,
I am thy Wigmore, Fraunce shall be thy Court;
How canst thou want millions of Pearle and gold,
When thou the Indies in thyne armes dost hold?

Thou art King Edward, or opinion fayles,
Longshanks begot thee when in youth he rang'd,
Thou art Carnaruan, thou the Prince of Wales,
And in thy Cradle falsely thou wert chang'd,
Hee Mortimer, and thou hast beene estrang'd:
Pardon me deere, what Mortimer sayd I,
Then should I love him, but my tongue doth lie,

As Fortune hath created him a King,
Had Nature made him valiant as thou art,
My soule had not beene tuch'd with torments sting,
Nor hadst thou now been plac'd so neere my hart;
But since by lot this falleth to thy part,
If such have wealth as lewdly will abuse it,
Let those enjoy it who can better use it.

Except to heaven, my hopes can clime no hier;
Now in mine armes had I my little boy,
Then had I all on earth I could desier,
The King's as he would be, God send him joy,
Now with his mynions let him sport and toy:
His lemman Spenser, and himselfe alone,
May sit and talke of Mistresse Gaueston.

When first I of that wanton King was woo'd,
Why camst thou not unto the Court of Fraunce?

Thou then alone should'st in my grace have stood,
O Mortimer, how good had been thy chaunce?
Then had I beene thine owne inheritance;
Now entrest thou by force, and holds by might,
And so intrud'st upon anothers right.

Honor that Idoll weomen so adore,
How many plagues hast thou in store to grieue us,
When in our selues we finde there yet is more
Then that bare word of maiestie can give us?
When of that comfort so thou canst depriue us,
Which with our selues oft sett'st us at debate,
And mak'st us beggers in our greatest state.

Even as a Trumpets lively-sounding voyce,
Tryps on the winds with many a dainty trick,
When as the speaking Ecchoes doe rejoyce,
So much delighted with the rethorick,
Seeming to make the heauie dull ayre quick;
With such rare musick in a thousand kayes,
Upon his hart-strings shee in consort playes.

On thys foundation whilst they firmely stand,
And as they wish, so fitly all things went,
No worse their warrant, then King Edwards hand,
Who his owne Bow to his destruction bent;
The course of things to fall in true consent,
Gives full assurance of the happy end,
On which their thoughts now carefully attend.

And sith in payment all for currant passe,
And theyr proceedings were allow'd for such,
Although this peace against her stomack was,
And yet imports the Princes strength so much,
To carry all things cleerly without tuch,
With seeming care doth seemingly effect,
What love commaunds, and greatnes should respect.

Charles waying well his lawfull Nephews right,
So mighty an Embassador as shee,
This meane to winne her grace in Edwards sight,
And so reclaime his vaine inconstancie,
With kindnes thus to conquer all these three,
What love the subjects to his Sister bore,
Heapes on desert, to make this much the more.

Her expedition, and thys great successe
Of after-good, still seeming to devine,

Carnaruan should by couenant release,
And to the Prince the Prouinces resigne,
Who dooing homage, should reenter Guyne,
Safe-conduct sent the King, to come with speed,
To seale in person what the Queene decreed.

But whilst he stood yet doubtfull what to doe,
The Spensers who his counsels chiefely guide,
Nor with theyr Soveraigne into Fraunce durst goe,
Nor in his absence durst at home abide:
His listning eares with such perswasions plyde,
As hee by them, to stay at home is wonne,
And with Commission to dispatch his Sonne.

Now till thys howre all joyes inwombed lay,
And in this howre now came they first to light,
Ad dayes to Months, and howres unto the day,
And as loue dyd, so make a treble night,
And whilst delight is rauish'd with delight,
Swound in these sweets, in pleasures pleasing paine,
And as they die, so brought to life againe.

Now Clowd-borne care, hence vanish for a time,
The Sunne ascending, hath the yeere renew'd,
And as the Halkes in hotest Sotherne clime,
Their halfe-sick hopes their crazed flags have mew'd,
A world of joyes their brests doe now include,
The thoughts whereof, thoughts quicknes doth benum,
In whose expression, pens and tongues be dumbe.

In fayre Lauinium, Troy is built againe,
And on thys shore her ruins are repard,
Nor Iunos hate such vigor doth retaine,
The Fates appeas'd who with theyr fortune squard,
The remnant of the shypwrackt nauie spard,
Though torne with tempests, yet ariu'd at last,
May sit and sing, and tell of sorrowes past.

If shee doe sit, he leanes on Cynthias throne,
If shee doe walke, he in the circle went,
If shee doe sport, he must be grac'd alone,
If shee discourse, he is the argument,
If shee devise, it is to his content:
From her proceeds the light he beares about him,
And yet she sets if once shee be without him.

Still with his eares his soveraigne Goddesse hears,
And with his eyes shee graciously doth see,

Still in her breast his secret thoughts she bears,
Nor can her tongue pronounce an I, but wee,
Thus two in one, and one in two they bee:
And as his soule possesseth head and hart,
Shee's all in all, and all in every part.

Like as a well-tund Lute thats tucht with skill,
In Musicks language sweetly speaking playne,
When every string it selfe with sound doth fill,
Taking their tones, and giuing them againe,
A diapazon heard in every strayne:
So their affections set in kayes so like,
Still fall in consort, as their humors strike.

Shee must returne, King Edwards will is so,
But soft a while, shee meaneth no such thing,
He's not so swift, but shee is twice as slowe,
No hast, but good, this message backe to bring,
Another tune he must be taught to sing:
Which to his hart more deadly is by far,
Then cryes of ghosts, or Mandrakes shreekings are.

Stapleton who had beene of their counsell long,
Or woonne with gifts, or else of childish feare,
Or mou'd in conscience with King Edwards wrong,
Or pittying him, or hate to them did beare,
Or of th'event that now he did dispaire:
This Bishop backe from Fraunce to Edward flewe,
And knowing all discovered all he knewe.

The platforme of this enterprize disclosd,
And Torltons drift by circumstances found,
With what conueyance all things are disposd,
The cunning usd in laying of the ground,
And with what Art, this curious trayle is woond:
Awakes the King, to see his owne estate,
When to prevent, he comes a day too late.

Isabell the time doth still and still reiorne,
Charles as a Brother with perswasions deales,
Edward with threats, doth hasten her retorne,
Pope Iohn, with Bulls and curses hard assailes,
Perswasions, curses, threats, no whit prevailes:
Chales, Edward, Iohn, Pope, Princes, doe your worst,
The Queene fares best, when she the most is curst.

The Spensers, who the French-mens humors felt,
And with their Soveraigne, had devisd the draught,

With Prince, and Peers, now under hand had delt,
In golden nets, who were alreadie caught,
And nowe King Charles, they have so throughlie wrought:
That he with sums, too slightly overwaid,
Poore Isabells hopes, now in the dust are layd.

Thou base desier, thou grave of all good harts,
Corsiue to kindnes, bawd to beastly will,
Monster of time, defrauder of desarts,
Thou plague, which doest both love and vertue kill,
Honours abuser, friendships greatest ill:
If curse in hell, there worse then other bee,
I pray that curse, may trebled light on thee.

Nor can all these amaze this mighty Queene,
Who with affliction, never was controld,
Never such courage in her sex was seene,
Nor was she cast in other womens mould,
But can endure warres, trauell, want, and cold:
Strugling with Fortune, nere with greefe opprest,
Most cheerefull still, when she was most distrest,

Thus she resolu'd, to leave ungratefull France,
And in the world her fortune yet to trye,
Chaunging the ayre, hopes time will alter chance,
As one whose thoughts with honors wings doe flye,
Her mighty mind, still scorning miserie:
Yet ere she went, her greeued hart to heale,
Shee rings King Charles, this dolefull parting peale.

Is this the trust I have repos'd (quoth shee)
And to this end to thee my griefes have told?
Is this the kindnes that thou offerest mee?
And in thy Country am I bought and sold?
In all this heate art thou become so cold?
Came I to Fraunce in hope to find a frend?
And now in thee have all my hopes their end?

Phillip (quoth shee) thy Father never was,
But some base peasant, or some slauish hind,
Never did Kingly Lyon get an Asse,
Nor cam'st thou of that Princely Eagles kind:
But sith thy hatefull cowardise I find,
Sinke thou, thy power, thy Country, ayde and all,
Thou barbarous Moore, thou most unnaturall.

Thou wert not Sonne unto the Queene my mother,
Nor wert conceiued in her sacred woombe,

Some misbegotten changeling, not my Brother,
O that thy Nurses armes had beene thy Toombe,
Or thy birth-day had beene the day of the doombe:
Never was Fortune with such error led,
As when shee plac'd a Crowne upon thy head.

And for my farewell this I prophecie,
That from my loynes, that glorious fruite shall spring,
Which shall tread downe that base posteritie,
And lead in tryumph thy succeeding King,
To fatall Fraunce, I as Sibilla sing:
Her Citties sackd, the ruine of her men,
When of the English, one shall conquer ten.

Beumount who had in Fraunce this shufling seene,
Whose soule with kindnes Isabell had wonne,
To flye to Henault, now perswades the Queene,
Assuring her what good might there be done,
Offering his Neece, unto the Prince her Sonne:
The onely meane, to bend his brothers might,
Against King Edward, and to back her right.

This worthy Lord, experienc'd long in armes,
Whom Isabell with many fauours grac'd,
Whose Princely blood, the brute of conquest warmes,
In whose great thoughts, the Queene was highly plac'd,
Greeuing to see her succours thus defac'd.
Hath cast this plot, which managed with heed,
Sith all doe fayle, should onely helpe at need.

Shee who but lately had her Ankors wayd,
And sawe the cloudes on every side to rise,
Nor now can stay, untill the streame be stayd,
Nor harbour till the cleering of the skies,
Who though she rou'd, the marke stil in her eyes,
Accepts his offer thankfully as one,
Succouring the poore in such affliction.

This courteous Earle, mou'd with her sad report,
Whose eares were drawne to her inchanting tong,
Traind up with her in Phillips royall Court,
And fully now confirmed in her wrong,
Her foes growe weake, her friends grow daily strong.
The Barrons oath, gag'd in her cause to stand,
The Commons word, the Cleargies helping hand.

All Covenants signd with wedlocks sacred seale,
In friendships bonds eternally to bind,

And all proceeding from so perfect zeale,
And suting right, with Henalts mighty mind,
What ease hereby, the Queene doth hope to find;
The sweet contentment of the lovely bride,
Young Edward pleasd, and joy on every side.

Now full seauen times, the Sunne his welked waine,
Had on the top of all the Tropick set,
And seaven times descending downe againe,
His fiery wheeles, had with the fishes wet,
Since malice first this mischiefe did beget:
In which so many courses hath beene runne,
As he that time celestiall signes hath done.

From Henalt now this great Bellona comes,
Glyding along fayre Belgias glassie maine,
Mazing the shores with noyse of thundring drums,
With her young Edward, Duke of Aquitayne,
The fatall scourges of King Edwards raigne:
Her Souldiour Beumount, and the Earle of Kent,
And Mortimer that mightie Malcontent.

Three thousand Souldiers mustred men in pay,
Of Almaynes, Swisers, trustie Henawers,
Of natiue English fled beyond the Sea,
Of fat-braind Fleamings, fishie Zelanders,
Edwards decreasing power, augmenting hers:
Her friends at home expect her comming in,
And new commotions every day begin.

The Coasts be daylie kept with watch and ward,
The Beacons burning, at thy foes discrie,
O had the love of Subjects beene thy guard,
T'ad beene t'effect, what thou didst fortifie,
But t'is thy houshold home-bred Enemie:
Nor Fort, nor Castell, can thy Countrey keepe,
When foes doe wake, and dreamed friends doe sleepe.

In vaine be armes, when heaven becomes a foe,
Kneele, weepe, intreat, and speake thy Deaths-man fayre,
The earth is armd unto thy overthrowe,
Goe pacifie the angrie powers by prayer,
Or if not pray, goe Edward and dispayre:
Thy fatall end, why doest thou this begin,
Locking Death out, thou keep'st destruction in.

A Southwest gale, for Harwich fitly blowes,
Blow not so fast, to kindle such a fier:

Whilst under saile, shee yet securely rowes,
Turne gentle wind, and force her to retyer,
But ô the winds, doe Edwards wrack conspyre,
For when the heavens are unto justice bent,
All things be turnd to our just punishment.

Shee is arriu'd in Orwells pleasant Roade,
Orwell thy name, or ill, or never was:
Why art thou not ore-burthend with thy loade?
Why sinck'st thou not under thys monstrous masse?
But what heaven will, that needs must come to passe.
That grieuous plague thou carriest on thy deepe,
Shall give just cause for many, streames to weepe.

Englands Earle-marshall, Lord of all that Coast,
With bells and bonfires welcoms her to shore,
Great Leicester next joyneth hoast to hoast,
The Cleargies power, in readines before,
Which every day increaseth more and more:
Upon the Church a great taxation layd,
For Armes, munition, mony, men, and ayd.

Such as too long had looked for this hower,
And in their brests imprisoned discontent,
Their wills thus made too powerful by their power
Whose spirits were factious, great, and turbulent,
Their hopes succesfull by this ill event,
Like to a thiefe that for his purpose lyes,
Take knowledge now of Edwards iniuries.

Young Prince of Wales, loe heere thy vertue lyes,
Soften thy Mothers flintie hart with teares,
Then wooe thy Father with those blessed eyes,
Wherein the image of himselfe appeares,
With thy soft hand softly uniting theirs:
With thy sweet kisses so them both beguile,
Untill they smyling weepe, and weeping smile.

Bid her behold that curled silken Downe,
Thy fayre smooth brow, in beauties fayrer pryme,
Not to be prest with a care-bringing Crowne,
Nor that with sorrowes wrinckled ere the time,
Thy feete too feeble to his seate to clime;
Who gave thee life, a crowne for thee did make,
Taking that Crowne, thou life from him doost take.

Looke on these Babes, the seales of plighted troth,
Whose little armes about your bodies cling,

These pretty imps, so deere unto you both,
Beg on their knees, their little hands do wring,
Queenes to a Queene, Kings kneele unto a King,
To see theyr comfort, and the crowne defac'd,
You fall to Armes, which have in armes embrac'd.

Subjects see these, and then looke backe on these,
Where hatefull rage with kindly nature striues,
And judge by Edward of your owne disease,
Chyldren by chyldren, by his wife your wiues,
Your state by his, in his life your owne lives,
And yeeld your swords, to take your deaths as due,
Then draw your swords, to spoyle both him and you.

From Edmondsbury now comes thys Lyonesse,
Under the Banner of young Aquitaine,
And downe towards Oxford doth herselfe adresse,
A world of vengeance wayting on her traine,
Heere is the period of Carnaruans raigne;
Edward thou hast, but King thou canst not beare,
Ther's now no King, but great King Mortimer.

Now friendles Edward followed by his foes,
Needes must he runne, the devill hath in chase,
Poore in his hopes, but wealthy in his woes,
Plenty of plagues, but scarcitie of grace,
Who wearied all, now wearieth every place;
No home at home, no comfort seene abroad,
His minde small rest, his body small aboad.

One scarce to him his sad discourse hath done
Of Henalts power, and what the Queene intends,
But whilst he speakes, another hath begun,
Another straight beginning where he ends,
Some of new foes, some of revolting frends;
These ended once, againe new rumors spred
Of many which rebell, of many fled.

Thus of the remnant of his hopes bereft,
Shee hath the sum, and hee the silly rest,
Towards Wales he flyes, of England being left,
To rayse an Armie there himselfe adrest,
But of his power shee fully is possest;
Shee hath the East, her rising there-withall,
And he the West, I there goes downe his fall.

What plagues doth Edward for himselfe prepare?
Alas poore Edward, whether doost thou flie?

Men change the ayre, but seldome change their care,
Men flie from foes, but not from miserie,
Griefes be long-liv'd, and sorrowes seldome die;
And whē thou feel'st thy conscience tuch'd with griefe,
Thy selfe pursues thy selfe, both rob'd and thiefe.

Towards Lundy, which in Sabryns mouth doth stand,
Carried with hope, still hoping to finde ease,
Imagining thys were his natiue Land,
Thys England: and Severne the narrow seas,
With this conceit (poore soule) himselfe doth please.
And sith his rule is over-rul'd by men,
On byrds and beasts he'll king it once agen.

Tis treble death a freezing death to feele,
For him, on whom the sunne hath ever shone,
Who hath been kneel'd unto, can hardly kneele,
Nor hardly beg which once hath been his owne,
A fearefull thing to tumble from a throne;
Fayne would he be king of a little Ile,
All were his Empyre bounded in a myle.

Aboard a Barke, now towards the Ile he sayles,
Thinking to find some mercy in the flood:
But see, the weather with such power prevailes,
Not suffring him to rule thys peece of wood;
Who can attaine, by heaven and earth with-stood?
Edward, thy hopes but vainly doe delude,
By Gods and men uncessantly pursu'd.

At length to land his carefull Barke he hales,
Beaten with stormes, ballast with misery,
Thys home-bred exile, on the Coast of Wales,
Unlike himselfe, with such as like him bee,
Spenser, Reading, Baldock, these haplesse three,
They to him subject, he subject to care,
And he and they, to murther subject are.

To ancient Neyth, a Castell strongly built,
Thether repayre thys forlorne banish'd crew,
Which holdeth them, but not contaynes theyr guilt,
There hid from eyes, but not from envies view,
Nor from theyr starrs themselves they yet with-drew,
Walls may awhile keepe out an enemie,
But never Castle kept out destenie.

Heere Fortune hath immur'd them in this hold,
Willing theyr poore imprisoned liberty,

Liuing a death, in hunger, want, and cold,
Whilst murtherous treason entreth secretly,
All lay on hands to punish cruelty;
And when even might is up unto the chin,
Weake frends become strong foes to thrust him in.

Melpomine, thou dolefull Muse be gone,
Thy sad complaints be matters farre too light,
Heere (now) come plagues beyond comparison.
You dreadfull Furies, visions of the night,
With gastly howling all approch my sight,
And let pale ghosts with sable Tapers stand,
To lend sad light to my more sadder hand.

Each line shall be a history of woe,
And every accent as a dead mans cry;
Now must my teares in such aboundance flow,
As doe the drops of fruitfull Castaly,
Each letter must containe a tragedy:
Loe, now I come to tell this wofull rest,
The drerest tale that ever pen exprest.

You sencelesse stones, as all prodigious,
Or things which of like solid substance be,
Sith thus in nature all grow monsterous,
And unto kinde contrary disagree,
Consume, or burne, or weepe, or sigh with mee,
Unlesse the earth hard-harted, nor can moane,
Makes steele and stones, more hard then steele and stone.

All-guiding heaven, which so doost still maintaine
What ere thou moou'st in perfect unitie,
And bynd'st all things in friendshyps sacred chayne,
In spotles and perpetuall amitie,
Which is the bounds of thy great Emperie;
Why sufferest thou the sacriligious rage,
Of thys rebellious, hatefull, yron age.

Now ruine raignes, God helpe the Land the while,
All prysons freed to make all mischiefes free,
Traytors and Rebels called from exile,
All things be lawfull, but what lawfull bee,
Nothing our owne, but our owne infamie:
Death, which ends care, yet carelesse of our death,
Who steales our joyes, but stealeth not our breath.

London which didst thys mischiefe first begin,
Loe, now I come thy tragedy to tell,

Thou art the first thats plagued for this sin,
Which first didst make the entrance to this hell,
Now death and horror in thy walls must dwell,
Which should'st have care thy selfe in health to keepe,
Thus turn'st the wolues amongst the carelesse sheepe.

O had I eyes, another Thames to weepe,
Or words expressing more, then words expresse,
O could my teares, thy great foundation steepe,
To moane thy pride, thy wastfull vaine excesse,
Thy gluttonie, thy youthfull wantonnesse:
But t'is thy sinnes, that to the heavens are fled,
Dissoluing clowdes of vengeance on thy head.

The place prophan'd, where God should be adord,
The stone remou'd, whereon our faith is grounded,
Aucthoritie is scornd, counsell abhord,
Religion so by foolish sects confounded,
Weake consciences by vaine questions wounded:
The honour due, to Magistrates neglected,
What else but vengeance can there be expected?

When fayth but faynd, a faith doth onely fayne,
And Church-mens lives, give Lay-men leave to fall,
The Ephod made a cloake to cover gayne,
Cunning auoyding what's canonicall,
Yet holines the Badge to beare out all:
When sacred things be made a merchandize,
None talke of texts, then ceaseth prophicies.

When as the lawes, doe once peruert the lawes,
And weake opinion guides the common weale,
Where doubts should cease, doubts rise in every clawse,
The sword which wounds, should be a salue to heale,
Oppression works oppression to conceale:
Yet being us'd, when needfull is the use,
Right clokes all wrongs, and covers all abuse,

Tempestious thunders, teare the fruitlesse earth,
The roring Ocean past her bounds to rise,
Death-telling apparisions, monstrous birth,
Th'affrighted heaven with comet-glaring eyes,
The ground, the ayre, all fild with prodigies:
Fearefull eclipses, fierie vision,
And angrie Planets in coniunction.

Thy channels serue for inke, for paper stones,
And on the ground, write murthers, incests, rapes,

And for thy pens, a heape of dead-mens bones,
Thy letters, ugly formes, and monstrous shapes;
And when the earths great hollow concaue gapes,
Then sinke them downe, least shee we live upon,
Doe leave our use, and flye subjection.

Virgine, but Virgine onely in thy name,
Now for thy sinne what murtherer shall be spent:
Blacke is my inke, but blacker is thy shame,
Who shall revenge? my Muse can but lament,
With hayre disheueld, words and tears halfe spent:
Poore rauish'd Lucrece stands to end her lyfe,
Whlist cruell Tarquin whets the angrie knyfe.

Thou wantst redresse, and tyrannie remorce,
And sad suspition dyes thy fault in graine,
Compeld by force, must be repeld by force,
Complaints no pardon, penance helpes not payne,
But blood must wash out a more bloody stayne:
To winne thine honour with thy losse of breath,
Thy guiltlesse lyfe with thy more guiltie death,

Thou art benumd, thou canst not feele at all,
Plagues be thy pleasures, feare hath made past feare,
The deadly sound of sinnes nile-thundering fall,
Hath tuned horror setled in thine eare,
Shreeks be the sweetest Musicke thou canst heare:
Armes thy attyer, and weapons all thy good,
And all the wealth thou hast, consist in blood.

See wofull Cittie, on thy ruin'd wall,
The verie Image of thy selfe heere see,
Read on thy gates in charrecters thy fall,
In famish'd bodies, thine Anatomie,
How like to them thou art, they like to thee:
And if thy teares have dim'd thy hatefull sight,
Thy buildings are one fier to give thee light.

For world that was, a wofull is, complayne,
When men might have been buried when they dyed,
When Children might have in their cradels layne,
When as a man might have enjoy'd his bride,
The Sonne kneeld by his Fathers death-bed side:
The lyuing wrongd, the dead no right (now) have,
The Father sees his Sonne to want a grave.

The poore Samarian almost staru'd for food,
Yet sawced her sweet Infants flesh with tears,

But thou in child with murther, long'st for blood,
Which thy wombe wanting, casts the fruite it bears,
Thy viperous brood, their lothsome prison teyrs.
Thou drinkst thy gore out of a dead-mans scull,
Thy stomack hungry, though thy gorge be full.

Is all the world in sencelesse slaughter dround?
No pittying hart? no hand? no eye? no eare?
None holds his sword from ripping of the wound,
No sparke of pittie, nature, love, nor feare;
Be all so mad, that no man can forbeare?
Will you incur the cruell Neros blame,
Thus to discover your owne Mothers shame?

The man who of the plague yet rauing lyes,
Heares yeelding gosts to give their latest grone,
And from his carefull window nought espyes,
But dead-mens bodies, others making moane,
No talke but Death, and execution.
Poore silly women from their houses fled,
Crying (ô helpe) my husbands murthered;

Thames turne thee backe to Belgias frothie mayne,
Fayre Tame and Isis, hold backe both your springs,
Nor on thy London spread thy siluer trayne,
Nor let thy Ships lay forth their silken wings,
Thy shores with Swans late dying Dirgies rings,
Nor in thy armes let her imbraced bee,
Nor smile on her which sadly weepes on thee.

Time end thy selfe here, let it not be sayd,
That ever Death did first begin in thee,
Nor let this slaunder to thy fault be layd,
That ages charge thee with impietie,
Least feare what hath beene, argue what may be:
And fashioning so a habite of the mind.
Make men no men, and alter humaine kind.

But yet this outrage hath but taken breath,
For pittie past, she meanes to make amends,
And more enrag'd, she doth return to death,
And next goes downe King Edward and his frends,
What she hath hoarded, now she franckly spends:
In such strange action as was never seene,
Clothing revenge in habite of a Queene.

Now Stapleton's thy turne, from France that fled,
The next the lot unto the Spensers fell,

Reding the Marshall, marshal'd with the dead,
Next is thy turne great Earle of Arundell,
Then Mochelden and wofull Daniell:
Who followed him in his lasciuious wayes,
Must goe before him to his blackest dayes,

Carnaruan by his Countrie-men betrayd,
And sent a Prisoner from his natiue Land,
To Knelworth poore King he is conuayd,
To th'Earle of Leister with a mighty band;
And now a present Parliament in hand,
Fully concluding what they had begunne,
T'uncrowne King Edward, and inuest his Sonne?

A scepter's lyke a pillar of great height,
Whereon a mighty building doth depend,
Which when the same is over-prest with weight,
And past his compasse, forc'd therby to bend,
His massie roofe down to the ground doth send:
Crushing the lesser props, and murthering all,
Which stand within the compasse of his fall.

Where vice is countenanc'd with nobilitie,
Arte cleane excluded, ignorance held in,
Blinding the world, with mere hipocrisie,
Yet must be sooth'd in all their slauish sinne,
Great malcontents to growe they then begin:
Nursing vile wits, to make them factious tooles,
Thus mighty men oft prooue the mightiest fooles.

The Senate wronged by the Senator,
And justice made injustice by delayes,
Next innouation playes the Orator,
Counsels uncounseld, Death defers no dayes,
And plagues, but plagues, alow no other playes:
And when one lyfe, makes hatefull many lives,
Caesar though Caesar, dyes with swords and kniues,

Now for the Cleargie, Peers, and Laietie,
Against the King must resignation make,
Th'elected Senate of the Emperie,
To Kenelworth are come, the Crowne to take,
Sorrowe hath yet but slept, and now awake:
In solemne sort each one doth take his place,
The partiall Judges of poore Edwards case.

From his imprisoning chamber, cloth'd in black,
Before the great assemblie he is brought,

A dolefull hearse upon a dead-mans back,
Whose heauie lookes, might tell his heauie thought,
Greefe neede no fayned action to be taught:
His Funerall solemniz'd in his cheere,
His eyes the Mourners, and his legs the Beere.

His fayre red cheeks clad in pale sheets of shame,
And for a dumbe shew in a swound began,
Where passion doth strange sort of passion frame,
And every sence a right Tragedian,
Exceeding farre the compasse of a man,
By use of sorrow learning nature arte,
Teaching Dispayre to act a lively part.

Ah Pitty, doost thou live, or art thou not?
Some say such sights, men unto flints have turned,
Or Nature, else thy selfe hast thou forgot?
Or is it but a tale, that men have mourned?
That water ever drown'd, or fire burned?
Or have teares left to dwell in humaine eyes,
Or ever man to pitty miseries?

Hee takes the Crowne, and closely hugs it to him,
And smiling in his greese he leanes upon it;
Then doth hee frowne because it would forgoe him,
Then softly stealing, layes his vesture on it;
Then snatching at it, loth to have forgone it,
Hee put it from him, yet hee will not so,
And yet retaines what fayne he would forgoe.

Like as a Mother over-charg'd with woe,
Her onely chylde now laboring in death,
Doing to helpe it, nothing yet can doe,
Though with her breath, she faine would give it breath,
Still saying, yet forgetting what shee sayth:
Even so with poore King Edward doth it fare,
Leauing his Crowne, the first-borne of his care.

In thys confused conflict of the minde,
Tears drowning sighes, and sighes confounding tears,
Yet when as neyther any ease could finde,
And extreame griefe doth somwhat harden feares,
Sorrow growes sencelesse when too much she bears,
Whilst speech & silence, striues which place should take,
With words halfe spoke, he silently bespake.

I clayme no Crowne, quoth he, by vise oppression,
Nor by the law of Nations have you chose mee,

My Fathers title groundeth my succession,
Nor in your power is cullor to depose mee,
By heavens decree I stand, they must dispose mee;
A lawles act, in an unlawfull thing,
With-drawes allegiance, but uncrownes no King.

What God hath sayd to one, is onely due,
Can I usurpe by tyrannizing might?
Or take what by your birth-right falls to you?
Roote out your houses? blot your honors light?
By publique rule, to rob your publique right?
Then can you take, what he could not that gave it,
Because the heavens commaunded I should have it.

My Lords, quoth hee, commend me to the King,
Heere doth he pause, fearing his tongue offended,
Even as in child-birth forth the word doth bring,
Sighing a full poynt, as he there had ended,
Yet striuing, as his speech he would have mended;
Things of small moment we can scarcely hold,
But griefes that tuch the hart, are hardly told.

Heere doth he weepe, as he had spoke in tears,
Calming this tempest with a shower of raine,
Whispering, as he would keepe it from his ears,
Doe my alegiance to my Soveraigne;
Yet at this word, heere doth he pause againe:
Yes say even so, quoth he, to him you beare it,
If it be Edward that you meane shall weare it.

Keepe hee the Crowne, with mee remaine the curse,
A haplesse Father, have a happy Sonne,
Take he the better, I endure the worse,
The plague to end in mee, in mee begun,
And better may he thriue then I have done;
Let him be second Edward, and poore I,
For ever blotted out of memorie.

Let him account his bondage from the day
That he is with the Diadem inuested,
A glittering Crowne doth make the haire soone gray,
Within whose circle he is but arested,
In all his feasts, hee's but with sorrowe feasted;
And when his feete disdaine to tuch the mold,
His head a prysoner, in a layle of gold.

In numbring of his subjects, numbring care,
And when the people doe with shouts begin,

Then let him thinke theyr onely prayers are,
That he may scape the danger he is in,
The multitude, be multitudes of sin;
And hee which first doth say, God saue the King,
Hee is the first doth newes of sorrow bring.

His Commons ills shall be his priuate ill,
His priuate good is onely publique care,
His will must onely be as others will:
Himselfe not as he is, as others are,
By Fortune dar'd to more then Fortune dare:
And he which may commaund an Empery,
Yet can he not intreat his liberty.

Appeasing tumults, hate cannot appease,
Sooth'd with deceits, and fed with flatteries,
Displeasing to himselfe, others to please,
Obey'd asmuch as he shall tyrannize,
Feare forcing friends, enforcing Enemies:
And when hee sitteth under his estate,
His foote-stoole danger, and his chayre is hate.

He King alone, no King that once was one,
A King that was, unto a King that is;
I am unthron'd, and hee enjoyes my throne,
Nor should I suffer that, nor he doe this,
He takes from mee what yet is none of his;
Young Edward clymes, old Edward falleth downe;
King'd and unking'd, he crown'd, farwell my crowne.

Princes be Fortunes chyldren, and with them,
Shee deales, as Mothers use theyr babes to still,
Unto her darling gives a Diadem,
A pretty toy, his humor to fulfill;
And when a little they have had theyr will,
Looke what shee gave, shee taketh at her pleasure,
Using the rod when they are out of measure.

But policie, who still in hate did lurke,
And yet suspecteth Edward is not sure,
Waying what blood with Leicester might worke,
Or else what friends his name might yet procure,
A guilty conscience never is secure;
From Leisters keeping cause him to be taken;
Alas poore Edward, now of all forsaken.

To Gurney and Matrauers he is given;
O let theyr act be odious to all ears,

And beeing spoke, stirre clowdes to cover heaven,
And be the badge the wretched murtherer bears,
The wicked oth whereby the damned swears:
But Edward, in thy hell thou must content thee,
These be the devils which must still torment thee.

Hee on a leane ilfauored beast is set,
Death upon Famine moralizing right;
His cheeks with tears, his head with raigne bewet,
Nights very picture, wandring still by night;
When he would sleep, like dreams they him affright;
His foode torment, his drinke a poysoned bayne,
No other comfort but in deadly paine.

And yet because they feare to have him knowne,
They shave away his princely tressed hayre,
And now become not worth a hayre ofs owne,
Body and fortune now be equall bare;
Thus voyde of wealth, ô were he voyde of care.
But ô, our joyes are shadowes, and deceaue us,
But cares, even to our deaths doe never leave us.

A silly Mole-hill is his kingly chayre,
With puddle water must he now be drest,
And his perfume, the lothsome fenny ayre,
An yron skull, a Bason sitting best,
A bloody workman, suting with the rest;
His lothed eyes, within thys filthy glas,
Truly behold how much deform'd hee was.

The drops which from his eyes abundance fall,
A poole of tears still rising by this rayne,
Even fighting with the water, and withall,
A circled compasse makes it to retaine,
Billow'd with sighes, like to a little maine;
Water with tears, contending whether should
Make water warme, or make the warme tears cold.

Vise Traytors, hold of your unhalowed hands,
The cruelst beast the Lyons presence fears:
And can you keepe your Soveraigne then in bands?
How can your eyes behold th'anoynteds tears?
Are not your harts even pearced through the ears?
The minde is free, what ere afflict the man,
A King's a King, doe Fortune what shee can.

Who's he can take what God himselfe hath given?
Or spill that life his holy spirit infused?

All powers be subject to the powers of heaven,
Nor wrongs passe unreveng'd, although excused,
Weepe Maiestie to see thy selfe abused;
O whether shall authoritie be take,
When shee herselfe, herselfe doth so forsake?

A wreath of hay they on his temples bind,
Which when he felt, (tears would not let him see,)
Nature (quoth he) now art thou onely kind,
Thou giu'st, but Fortune taketh all from mee,
I now perceaue, that were it not for thee:
I should want water, clothing for my brayne,
But earth gives hay, and mine eyes give me rayne.

My selfe deform'd, lyke my deformed state,
My person made like to mine infamie,
Altring my fauour, could you alter fate,
And blotting beautie, blot my memorie,
You might flye slaunder, I indignitie:
My golden Crowne, tooke golden rule away,
A Crowne of hay, well sutes a King of hay.

Yet greeu'd agayne, on nature doth complayne,
Nature (sayth he) ô thou art just in all,
Why should'st thou then, thus strengthen me agayne,
To suffer things so much unnaturall?
Except thou be pertaker in my fall:
And when at once so many mischiefes meete,
Mak'st poyson nuterment, and bitter sweete.

And now he thinks he wrongeth Fortune much,
Who giveth him this great preheminence,
For since by fate his myseries be such,
Her worser name hath taught him pacience,
For no offence, he taketh as offence:
Crost on his back, and crosses in the brest,
Thus is he crost, who never yet was blest.

To Berckley thus they lead this wretched King,
The place of horror which they had fore-thought,
O heavens why suffer you so vile a thing,
And can behold, this murther to be wrought,
But that your wayes are all with judgement frought:
Now entrest thou, poore Edward to thy hell,
Thus take thy leave, and bid the world farewell.

O Berckley, thou which hast beene famous long,
Still let thy walls shreeke out a deadly sound,

And still complayne thee of thy greeuous wrong,
Preserue the figure of King Edwards wound,
And keepe their wretched footsteps on the ground:
That yet some power againe may give them breath,
And thou againe mayst curse them both to death.

The croking Rauens hideous voyce he hears,
Which through the Castell sounds with deadly yells,
Imprinting strange imaginarie fears,
The heauie Ecchoes lyke to passing bells,
Chyming far off his dolefull burying knells:
The iargging Casements which the fierce wind dryues,
Puts him in mind of fetters, chaynes, and gyues.

By silent night, the ugly shreeking Owles,
Lyke dreadfull Spirits with terror doe torment him,
The envious dogge, angry with darcknes howles,
Lyke messengers from damned ghosts were sent him,
Or with hells noysome terror to present him:
Under his roofe the buzzing night-Crow sings,
Clapping his windowe with her fatall wings.

Death still prefigur'd in his fearefull dreames,
Of raging Feinds, and Goblins that he meets,
Of falling downe from steepe-rocks into streames
Of Toombs, of Graves, of Pits, of winding sheets,
Of strange temptations and seducing sprits:
And with his cry awak'd, calling for ayde,
His hollowe voyce doth make him selfe afrayd.

Oft in his sleepe he sees the Queene to flye him,
Sterne Mortimer pursue him with his sword,
His Sonne in sight, yet dares he not come nigh him,
To whom he calls, who aunswereth not a word,
And lyke a monster wondred and abhord:
Widowes and Orphans following him with cryes,
Stabbing his hart, and scratching out his eyes.

Next comes the vision of his bloody raigne,
Masking along with Lancasters sterne ghost,
Of eight and twentie Barrons hang'd and slayne,
Attended with the rufull mangled host,
At Burton and at Borough battell lost:
Threatning with frownes, and trembling every lim,
With thousand thousand curses cursing him.

And if it chaunce that from the troubled skyes,
Some little brightnes through the chinks give light,

Straight waies on heaps the thrunging clouds doe rise,
As though the heaven were angry with the night.
Deformed shadowes glimpsing in his sight:
As though darcknes, for she more darcke would bee,
Through these poore Crannells forc'd her selfe to see,

Within a deepe vault under where he lay,
Under buried filthie carcasses they keepe,
Because the thicke walls hearing kept away,
His feeling feeble, seeing ceas'd in sleepe;
This lothsome stinck comes from this dungeon deepe,
As though before they fully did decree,
No one sence should from punishment be free.

Hee haps our English Chronicle to find,
On which to passe the howers he falls to reed,
For minuts yet to recreate his mind,
If any thought one uncar'd thought might feed,
But in his breast new conflicts this doth breed:
For when sorrowe, is seated in the eyes,
What ere we see, increaseth miseries.

Opening the Booke, he chaunced first of all
On conquering Williams glorious comming in,
The Normans rising, and the Bryttains fall,
Noting the plague ordyan'd for Harolds sinne,
How much, in how short time this Duke did winne;
Great Lord (quoth hee) thy conquests plac'd thy throne,
I to mine owne, have basely lost mine owne.

Then comes to Rufus a lasciuious King,
Whose lawlesse rule on that which he enjoy'd,
A sodaine end unto his dayes doth bring,
Himselfe destroy'd in that which he destroy'd,
None moane his death, whose lyfe had all anoy'd:
Rufus (quoth he) thy fault far lesse then mine,
Needs must my plague be far exceeding thine.

To famous Bewclarke studiouslie he turnes.
Who from Duke Robert doth the scepter wrest,
Whose eyes put out, in flintie Cardiffe mornes,
In Palestine who bare his conquering crest,
Who though of Realmes, of same not dispossest:
In all afflictions this may comfort thee,
Onely my shame in death remaines (quoth hee.)

Then comes he next to Stephens troublous state,
Plagu'd with the Empresse, in continuall warre,

Yet with what patience he could beare his hate,
And lyke a wise-man rule his angry starre,
Stopping the wheele of Fortunes giddie carre:
O thus (quoth he) had gracelesse Edward done,
He had not now beene Subject to his Sonne.

Then to Henry Plantagine he goes,
Two Kings at once, two Crown'd at once doth find,
The roote from whence so many mischiefes rose,
The Fathers kindnes makes the Sonne unkind,
Th'ambitious Brothers to debate inclind:
Thou crown'st thy Sonne, yet liuing still do'st raigne,
Mine uncrownes me (quoth he) yet am I slaine.

Then of couragious Lyon-hart he reeds,
The Souldans terror, and the Pagans wrack,
The Easterne world fild with his glorious deeds,
Of Ioppas siege, of Cipres wofull sack,
Richard (quoth hee) turning his dull eyes back:
Thou did'st in height of thy felicitie,
I in the depth of all my miserie.

Then by degrees to sacriligious Iohn,
Murthering young Arthur, hath usurp'd his right,
The Cleargies curse, the poors oppression,
The greeuous crosses that on him did light,
To Rooms proud yoke yeelding his awfull might:
Even by thy end (he sayth) now Iohn I see,
Gods judgements thus doe justly fall on mee.

Then, to long-raigning Winchester his Sonne,
With whom his people bloody warre did wage,
And of the troubles in his time begunne,
The head-strong Barrons wrath, the Commons rage.
And yet how he these tumults could aswage:
Thou livest long, (quoth he) longer thy name,
And I dye soone, yet over-live my fame,

Then to great Longshanks mighty victories,
Who in the Orcads fix'd his Countries mears,
And dar'd in fight our fayths proud Enemies,
Which to his name eternall Trophies rears,
Whose gracefull fauors yet faire England wears:
Bee't deadly sinne (quoth he) once to defile,
This Fathers name with me a Sonne so vile.

Following the leafe, he findeth unawars,
What day young Edward Prince of Wales was borne,

Which Letters seeme lyke Magick Charrecters,
Or to dispight him they were made in scorne,
O let that name (quoth he) from Books be torne:
Least that in time, the very greeued earth,
Doe curse my Mothers woombe, and ban my birth.

Say that King Edward never had such child,
Or was devour'd as hee in cradle lay,
Be all men from my place of birth exil'd,
Let it be sunck, or swallowed with some sea,
Let course of yeeres devoure that dismall day,
Let all be doone that power can bring to passe,
Onely be it forgot that ere I was.

The globy tears impearled in his eyes,
Through which as glasses hee is forc'd to looke,
Make letters seeme as circles which arise,
Forc'd by a stone within a standing Brooke,
And at one time, so diuers formes they tooke,
Which like to vglie Monsters doe affright,
And with their shapes doe terrifie his sight.

Thus on his carefull Cabin falling downe,
Enter the Actors of his tragedy,
Opening the doores, which made a hallow soune,
As they had howl'd against theyr crueltie,
Or of his paine as they would prophecie;
To whom as one which died before his death,
He yet complaynes, whilst paine might lend him breath.

O be not Authors of so vile an act,
To bring my blood on your posteritie,
That Babes even yet unborne doe curse the fact,
I am a King, though King of miserie,
I am your King, though wanting Maiestie:
But he who is the cause of all this teene,
Is cruell March the Champion of the Queene.

He hath my Crowne, he hath my Sonne, my wyfe,
And in my throne tryumpheth in my fall,
Is't not inough but he will have my lyfe?
But more, I feare that yet this is not all,
I thinke my soule to judgement he will call:
And in my death his rage yet shall not dye,
But persecute me so, immortallie.

And for you deadly hate me, let me live,
For that aduantage angrie heaven hath left,

Fortune hath taken all that she did give;
Yet that revenge should not be quite bereft,
Shee leaves behind this remnant of her theft:
That miserie should find that onely I,
Am far more wretched then is miserie.

Betwixt two beds these devils straight enclos'd him,
Thus done, uncovering of his secrete part,
When for his death they fitly had disposd him,
With burning yron thrust him to the hart.
O payne beyond all paine, how much thou art!
Which words, as words, may verbally confesse,
But never pen precisely could expresse.

O let his tears even freezing as they light,
By the impression of his monstrous payne,
Still keepe this odious spectacle in sight,
And shew the manner how the King was slaine,
That it with ages may be new againe;
That all may thether come that have beene told it,
And in that mirror of his griefes behold it.

Still let the building sigh his bitter grones,
And with a hollow cry his woes repeate,
That sencelesse things even mouing sencelesse stones,
With agonizing horror still may sweat;
And as consuming in their furious heate,
Like boyling Cauldrons be the drops that fall,
Even as that blood for vengeance still did call,

O let the wofull Genius of the place,
Still haunt the pryson where his life was lost:
And with torne hayre, and swolne il-favored face,
Become the guide to his revengefull ghost,
And night and day still let them walke the Coast:
And with incessant howling terrifie,
Or mooue with pitty all that travell by.

True vertuous Lady, now of mirth I sing,
To sharpen thy sweet spirit with some delight,
And somwhat slack this mellancholie string,
Whilst I of love and tryumphs must indite,
Too soone againe of passion must I write.
Of Englands wonder, now I come to tell,
How Mortimer first rose, when Edward fell.

Downe lesser lights, the glorious Sunne doth clime
His joyfull rising is the worlds proude morne;

Now is he got betwixt the wings of Tyme,
And with the tyde of Fortune forwards borne,
Good starrs assist his greatnes to subborne;
Who have, decreed his raigning for a while,
All laugh on him, on whom the heavens doe smile.

The pompous sinode of these earthly Gods,
At Salsbury, appointed by their King,
To set all even which had been at ods,
And into fashion, their dissignes to bring,
That peace might now frō their proceedings spring,
And to establish what they had begun,
Under whose cullour mighty things were done.

Heere Mortimer is Earle of March created,
Thys honor added to his Barronie,
And unto fame heere is he consecrated,
That titles might his greatnes dignifie,
As for the rest, he easely could supply
Who knew a kingdom to her lap was throwne,
Which hauing all, would never starue her owne.

A pleasing calme hath smooth'd the troubled sea,
The prime brought on with gentle falling showers,
The misty breake yet proues a goodly day;
And on their heads since heaven her largesse powers,
That onely ours, which we doe use as ours:
Pleasures be poore, and our delights be dead,
When as a man doth not enjoy the head.

Tyme wanting bounds, still wanteth certainty,
Of dangers past, in peace wee love to heare,
Short is the date of all extreamity,
Long wished things a sweet delight doth beare,
Better forgoe our joyes then still to feare:
Fortune her gifts in vaine to such doth gyue,
As when they live, seeme as they did not live.

Now stand they like the two starre-fixed Poles,
Betwixt the which the circling Spheres doe moue,
About whose Axeltree thys fayre Globe roules,
Which that great Moover by his strength doth shoue,
Yet every poynt still ending in theyr love;
For might is ever absolute alone,
When of two powers there's true coniunction.

The King must take, what by theyr power they give,
And they protect what serues for theyr protection,

They teach to rule, whilst he doth learne to live,
T' whom all be subject, lives in theyr subjection,
Though borne to rule, yet crown'd by their election,
Th'alegiance which to Edward doth belong,
Doth make theyr faction absolutely strong.

Twelue guide the King, his power theyr powers consist,
Peers guide the King, they guide both King and Peers,
Ill can the Brooke his owne selfe-streame resist,
Theyr aged counsell, to his younger yeeres,
Young Edward vowes, and all the while he steers;
Wel might we think the man were more then blind,
Which wanted Sea roomth, and could rule the wind.

In lending strength, theyr strength they still retaine,
Building his force, theyr owne they so repare,
Under his raigne, in safety they doe raigne,
They give a kingdome, and doe keepe the care,
They who aduenture, must the booty share,
A Princes wealth in spending still doth spred,
Like to a Poole with many fountaines fed.

They sit at ease, though he sit in the throne,
He shaddowes them who his supporters be,
And in diuision they be two for one,
An Empyre now must thus berul'd by three,
What they make free, they challenge to be free;
The King enjoyeth, but what they lately gave,
They priuiledg'd to spend, leave him to saue.

Nine-score brave Knights belonging to his Court
At Notingham, which all the Coast commaunds,
All parts pay trybute, honor to his port,
Much may he doe which hath so many hands,
This rocke-built Castell, over-looks the Lands:
Thus lyke a Gyant, still towards heaven doth ryse,
And fayne would cast the Rocks against the skyes.

Where ere he goes there pompe in tryumph goes,
Over his head Fame soring still doth flye,
Th'earth in his presence decks her selfe in showes,
And glory sits in greatest Maiestie,
Aboundance there doth still in Child-bed lye:
For where Fortune her bountie will bestowe,
There heaven and earth must pay what she doth owe.

In Notingham, the Norths great glorious eye,
Crowne of the beautious branch-embellish'd soyle,

The throne emperiall of his Emperie,
His resting place, releever of his boyle,
Here he enjoyes his never-prized spoyle:
There lyuing in a world of all delight,
Beheld of all, and hauing all in sight.

Here all along the flower-enameld vales,
Cleere Trent upon the pearly sand doth slide,
And to the Meadowes telling wanton tales,
Her christall lims lasciuiously in pride,
With thousand turnes shee casts from side to side:
As loth shee were the sweet soyle to forsake,
And throw her selfe into the German lake.

Whence great hart-harboring Sherwood wildly roues,
Whose leauie Forrests garlanding her Towers,
Shadowing the small Brooks with her Ecchoing groues,
Whose thick-plashd sides repulse the Northerne showers,
Where Nature sporting in her secret Bowers:
This strong built Castell hurketh in her shade,
As to this end she onely had beene made.

There must the glorious Parliament be held,
Earth must come in, when awfull heaven doth send,
For whether loue his powerfull selfe doth weld,
Thether all powers them selues must wholly bend,
Whose hand holds thunder, who dare him offend?
And where proud conquest keepeth all in awe,
Kings oft are forc'd in seruile yokes to drawe.

Heere sit they both under the rich estate,
Yet neither striue the upper hand to get,
In pompe and power both equall at a rate,
And as they came, so are they friendly set,
He entreth first, which first in entring met;
A King at least the Earle of March must be,
Or else the maker of a King is hee.

Perhaps, he with a smyle the King will grace,
His knees growe stiffe, they have forgot to bow,
And if he once have taken up his place,
Edward must come, if he his will would know,
A foote out of his seate he cannot goe;
Thys small word subject, pricks him like a sting,
My Empyres Colleage, or my fellow King.

O had felicity feeling of woe,
Or could on meane but moderatly seede,

Or would looke downe the way that he must goe,
Or could abstaine from what diseases breede,
To stop the wound before to death he bleede,
Warre should not fill Kings Pallaces with moane,
Nor perrill come when tis least thought upon.

Ambition with the Eagle loves to build,
Nor on the Mountayne dreads the winters blast,
But with selfe-soothing doth the humor guild,
With arguments correcting what is past,
Fore-casting Kingdomes, daungers unforecast:
Leauing this poore word of content to such,
Whose earthly spirits have not his fierie touch.

But pleasures never dine but on excesse,
Whose dyet made to drawe on all delight,
And overcome in that sweet drunkennes,
His appetite maintayned by his sight,
Strengthneth desier, but ever weakneth might:
Untill this ulcer ripening to a head,
Vomits the poyson which it nourished.

Even as a flood swelling beyond his bounds,
Doth over-presse the channell where he flowd,
And breaking forth, the neighbour Meadows drowns,
That of him selfe, him selfe doth quite unload,
Dispearcing his owne greatnes all abroad:
Spending the store he was maintayned by,
Empties his Brooke, and leaves his Channell dry.

Upon this Subject, envie might devise,
Here might she prooue her mischeese-working wings,
An obiect for her ever-waking eyes,
Wherein to stick a thousand deadly stings,
A ground whereon to build as many things:
For where our actions measure no regard,
Our lawlesse will is made his owne reward.

Here vengeance calls destruction up from hell,
Coniuring mischeese to devise a curse,
Increasing that, which more and more did swell,
Adding to ill, to make this euill worse,
Whilst hatefull pride becomes ambitions nurse:
T'is incident to those whom many feare,
Many to them more greeuous hate doe beare.

And now those fewe which many tears had spent,
And long had wept on olde King Edwards grave,

Find some begin to pittie their lament,
Wishing the poore yet some redresse might have,
Revenge cannot denie what death doth craue:
Opening their cares what so abhord their eyes,
Ill will too soone regardeth envies cryes.

Time calls account of what before is past,
All thrust on mallice pressing to be hard,
Unto misfortune all men goe too fast,
Seldome, aduantage is in wrongs debard,
Nor in revenge a meane is never spard:
For when once pryde but poynteth towards his fall,
He bears a sword to wound him selfe with all.

Edward whose shoulders now were taught to peyze,
Briarius burthen, which opprest him so,
His current stop'd with these outragious Seas,
Whose gulfe receau'd the tyde should make him flowe,
This Rocke cast in the way where he must goe:
That honor brooks, no fellowship hath tryde,
Nor never Crowne Corriuall could abyde.

Some urge that March, meaning by blood to rise,
First cut off Kent, fearing he might succeed,
Trayning the King to what he did devise,
Lymming in cullors this unlawfull deed,
And to his owne, the royall blood to weed:
Thus every strawe prooues fewell to the fier,
When counsell doth concurre with our desier.

All fence the tree which serueth for a shade,
Whose great growne body doth repulse the wind,
Untill his wastfull branches doe invade,
The straighter plants, and them in pryson bind,
Then lyke a foule devower of his kind:
Unto his roote all put their hands to hewe,
Whose roomth but hinder other which would grow.

Greatnes, lyke to the Sunnes reflecting powers,
The fen-bred vapours naturally exhales,
And is the cause that oft the evening lowers,
When foggie mists enlarge their duskie failes,
That his owne beames, he in the clouds impales:
And eyther must extinguish his owne light,
Or by his vertue cause his propper night.

Of winter thus whilst they prognosticate,
He hath the Sommer, and a fruitfull yeare,

And still is soothed by his flattering fate,
For still the starre which guides him doth appeare;
Hee looks far off, yet sees not daunger neare:
For oft we see before a sodaine shower,
The sunne shines hott'st, and hath the greatest power.

Now sphears with Musick make a new worlds birth,
Bring on againe olde Saturns golden raigne,
Renewe this wearie barren-wombed earth,
And rayse aloft the sunnes declyning wayne,
And by your power make all things young agayne:
Orpheus, once more to Thebes olde Forrests bring,
Drinke Nectar, whilst the Gods are banquetting.

Within this Castell had the Queene devisd,
A stately Chamber with the pensill wrought,
Within whose compasse was imparadizd,
What ever Arte or rare inuention taught,
As well might seeme far to exceed all thought:
That were the thing on earth to moue delight,
He should not want it to content his sight.

Heere Phoebus clipping Hiacynthus stood,
Whose lyues last drops, his snowie breast imbrewe,
Mixing his christall tears with purple blood,
As were it blood or tears, none scarcely knewe,
Yet blood and tears, one from the other drewe:
The little wood-nimphs chasing him with balme,
To rayse this sweet Boy from this deadly qualme.

Here lyes his Lute, his Quiver, and his bowe,
His golden mantle on the greene-spred ground,
That from the things themselves none could them know,
The sledge so shadowed, still seem'd to rebound,
Th'wound beeing made, yet still to make a wound:
The purple flower with letters on the leaves,
Springing that Nature, oft her selfe deceaues.

The milke-white Heifor, Io, Ioues faire rape,
Viewing her new-ta'en figure in a Brooke,
The water seeming to retayne the shape,
Which lookes on her, as shee on it doth looke,
That gazing eyes oft-times them selves mistooke:
By prospectiue devis'd that looking nowe,
Shee seem'd a Mayden, then againe a Cowe.

Then Mercurie amidst his sweetest joyes,
Sporting with Hebe by a Fountayne brim,

Clipping each other with lasciuious toyes,
And each to other lapped lim to lim,
On tufts of flowers which loosely seeme to swim:
Which flowers in sprinckled drops doe still appeare,
As all their bodies so embraudered were.

Heere clyffy Cynthus, with a thousand byrds,
Whose checkerd plumes adorne his tufted crowne,
Under whose shadow graze the stragling heards,
Out of whose top, the fresh springs trembling downe,
Duly keepe time with theyr harmonious sowne.
The Rock so lively done in every part,
As arte had so taught nature, nature arte.

The naked Nymphes, some up, some downe discending.
Small scattering flowers one at another flung,
With pretty turns their lymber bodies bending,
Cropping the blooming branches lately sprong,
Which on the Rocks grewe heere and there among.
Some combe theyr hayre, some making garlands by,
As liuing, they had done it actually.

And for a trayle, Caisters siluer Lake,
Whose heards of Swanns sit pruning on a row,
By their much whitenes, such reflection make,
As though in Sommer had been falne a snow,
Whose streame an easie breath doth seeme to blowe;
Which on the sparkling gravell runns in purles,
As though the waues had been of siluer curles.

Here falls proude Phaeton, tumbling through the clowds,
The sunny Palfreys have their traces broke,
And setting fire upon the welked shrowds,
Now through the heaven flye gadding from the yoke,
The Sphears all reeking with a mistie smoke,
Drawne with such life, as some did much desire
To warme themselves, some frighted with the fire.

And Drencht in Po, the Riuer seemes to burne,
His wofull sisters, mourning there he sees,
Trees unto women seeme themselves to turne,
Or rather women turned into trees,
Drops from their boughs, or tears fall from their eyes,
That fire seem'd to be water, water flame,
Eyther or neyther, and yet both the same.

A stately Bed under a golden tree,
Whose broad-leau'd branches covering over all,

Spread their large Armes like to a Canapy,
Dubbling themselves in their lasciuious fall,
Upon whose top the flying Cupids spraule,
And some, at sundry cullored byrds doe shute,
Some swaruing up to get the golden fruite.

A counterpoynt of Tyssue, rarely wrought,
Like to Arachnes web, of the Gods rape,
Which with his lifes strange history is wrought,
The very manner of his hard escape,
From poynt to poynt, each thing in perfect shape,
As made the gazers thinke it there was done,
And yet time stayd in which it was begun.

During thys calme, is gather'd that black showre,
Whose uglie clowde the clyme had over-spred,
And now drawes on that long death-dating howre,
His fatall starre now hangeth o're his head,
His fortunes sunne downe towards the evening fled,
For when we thinke we most in safety stand,
Great'st dangers then are ever near'st at hand.

And Edward sees no meanes can ever boote,
Unlesse thys head-strong course he may restraine,
And must pluck up these mischiefs by the roote,
Els spred so farre, might easely grow againe,
And end theyr raigne, if he doe meane to raigne;
The Common-weale to cure, brought to that passe,
Which like a many-headed Monster was.

But sith he finds the danger to be such,
To bring this Beare once bayted to the slake,
And that he feeles the forwardest to gruch,
To take in hand this sleeping dog to wake,
He must fore-think of some such course to take,
By which he might his purpose thus effect,
And hurt him most, where he might least suspect.

A trenched vault deepe in the earth is found,
Whose hollownes, like to the Sleep-gods Cell,
With strange Meanders turneth under ground,
Where pitchy darknes ever-more doth dwell,
As well might be an entrance into hell.
Which Archyteckts, to serue the Castell made,
When as the Dane with warrs did all invade.

Heere silent night, as in a pryson shrowded,
Wandreth about within thys mazed roome,

With filthy fogs, and earthly vapors clowded,
As shee were buried in this cliffy toombe,
Or yet unborne within the earths great woombe.
A dampy breath comes from the moysted vaines,
As shee had sigh'd through trouble in her paines.

Now on a long this cranckling path doth keepe,
Then by a rock turnes up another way,
Then rising up, shee poynteth towards the deepe,
As the ground leuell, or unleuell lay,
Nor in his course keepes any certaine stay,
Till in the Castell in a secret place,
He suddainly unmaske his duskie face.

The King now with a strong selected crue,
Of such as he with his intent acquainted,
And well affected to thys action knew,
Nor in revenge of Edward never fainted,
Whose loyall fayth had never yet beene tainted,
This Labyrinth dertermins to assay,
To rouze the beast which kept him thus at bay.

The blushing Sunne, plucks in his smyling beames,
Making his steeds to mend theyr wonted pace,
Till plunging downe into the Ocean streames,
There in the frothy waues he hides his face,
Then reynes them in, more then his usuall space,
And leaves foule darknes to possesse the skyes,
A time most fit for fouler tragedies.

With Torches now they enter on his Caue,
As night were day, and day were turnd to night,
Damp'd with the soyle one to the other gave,
Light hating darknes, darknes hating light,
As enemies, each with the other fight;
And each confounding other, both appeare,
As darknes light, and light but darknes were.

The craggy cleeues, which crosse them as they goe,
Seeme as their passage they would have denied,
And threatning them, their iourney to for-slowe,
As angry with the path that was their guide,
Cursing the hand which did them first devide,
Theyr combrous falls and risings seem'd to say,
Thys wicked action could not brooke the day.

These gloomy Lamps, by which they on were led,
Making theyr shaddowes follow at theyr back,

Which like to Mourners, waite upon the dead,
And as the deed, so are they ugly black,
Like to the dreadfull Images of wrack;
These poore dym-burning lights, as all amazed,
As those deformed shades whereon they gazed.

Theyr clattering Armes, their Masters seeme to chyde,
As they would reason wherefore they should wound.
And striking with the poynts from side to side,
As they were angry with the hollow ground,
Whose stony roofe lock'd in their dolefull found:
And hanging in the creeks, draw backe againe,
As willing them from murther to refraine.

Now, after masks and gallant revelings,
The Queene unto the Chamber is with-drawne,
To whom a cleer-voyc'd Eunuch playes and sings;
And underneath a Canapy of Lawne,
Sparkling with pearle, like to the cheerfull dawne,
Leaning upon the breast of Mortimer,
Whose voice more then the musick pleasd her eare.

A smock wrought with the purest Affrick silke,
A worke so fine, as might all worke refine,
Her breast like strains of violets in milk,
O be thou hence-forth Beauties liuing shrine,
And teach things mortall to be most diuine.
Enclose Love in thys Labyrinth about,
Where let him wander still, yet ne're get out.

Her golden hayre, ah gold, thou art too base,
Were it not sinne but once to name it hayre,
Falling as it would kisse her fairer face,
But no word fayre enough for thing so fayre,
Inuention is too bare, to paynt her bare;
But where the pen fayles, Pensill cannot show it,
Nor can be knowne, unlesse the minde doe knowe it.

Shee layes those fingers on his manly cheeke,
The Gods pure scepters, and the darts of love,
Which with one tuch might make a Tyger meeke,
Or might an Atlas easely remoue:
That lilly hand, rich Natures wedding glove,
Which might beget life where was never none,
And put a spirit into the hardest stone.

The fire of precious wood, the lights perfume,
Whose perfect cleernes, on the painting shone,

As every thing with sweetnes would consume,
And every thing had sweetnes of his owne,
The smell where-with they liv'd, & alwaies growne,
That light gave cullour on each thing it fell,
And to that cullour, the perfume gave smell.

Upon the sundry pictures they devise,
And from one thing they to an other runne,
Now they commend that body, then those eyes,
How well that byrd, how well that flower was done,
The lively counterfetting of that sunne:
The cullors, the conceits, the shadowings,
And in that Arte a thousand sundrie things.

Looking upon proud Phaeton wrapd in fier,
The gentle Queene doth much bewaile his fall,
But Mortimer more praysing his desier,
To loose his lyfe or else to governe all:
And though (quoth he) he now be Fortunes thrall,
This must be sayd of him when all is done,
Hee perrish'd in the Chariot of the Sunne.

Glaunsing upon Ixion, shee doth smile,
Who for his Iuno tooke the cloud amisse;
Madam (quoth hee) thus women can beguile,
And oft we find in love, this error is,
Why friend (quoth shee) thy hap is lyke to his:
That booteth not (quoth he) were he as I,
Ioue would have beene in monstrous jealousie.

 (Shee sayth) Phoebus is too much forc'd by Art,
Nor can shee find how his imbraces bee:
But Mortimer now takes the Paynters part,
Tis even thus great Empresse, so (quoth hee)
Thus twyne their armes, and thus their lips you see:
You Phoebus are, poore Hiacinthus I,
Kisse mee till I revive, and now I die.

By this into the uttermost stately hall,
Is rudely entred this disordred rout,
And they within suspecting least of all,
Prouide no guard to watch on them without,
Thus danger falls oft-times, when least we doubt:
In perrill thus we thinke our selves most sure,
And oft in death fond men are most secure.

His trustie Neuill, and young Turrington,
Courting the Ladies, frolick voyd of feare,

Staying delights whilst time away doth runne,
What rare Emprezas hee and he did beare,
Thus in the Lobby whilst they sporting weare:
Assayld on sudaine by this hellish trayne,
Both in the entrance miserably slayne.

Even as from snow-topd Skidos frostie cleeues,
Some Norway Haggard, to her pitch doth tower,
And downe amongst the moore-bred Mallard driues,
And through the aire, right down the wind doth scower,
Commaunding all that lye within her power:
Even such a skreame is hard within the vault,
Made by the Ladies at the first assault.

March hath no armes, but the Queene in his armes,
To fayre a sheeld to beare their fouler blowes,
Enchayning his strong armes, in her sweet armes,
Inclosing them which oft did her inclose,
O had he had but weapons lyke his woes:
Her presence had redoubled then his might,
To lyue and dye both in his soueraigns sight.

Villians (quoth hee) I doe protect the King,
Why Centaure-lyke doe you disturbe me this,
And interrupt the Gods at banquetting,
Where sacred Himen ever present is,
And pleasures are imparadizd in blis:
Where all they powers, their earthly heaven would take,
If heere on earth they their abode should make.

Her presence pardons the offenders ill,
And makes the basest earthly thing diuine,
Ther's no decree can countermaund her will,
Shee like the Sunne, doth blesse where she doth shine,
Her Chamber is the most unspotted shrine:
How sacriligiously dare you despise,
And thus prophane these halowed liberties.

But Edward, if this enterprize be thine,
And thou an Actor heere do'st play thy part,
I tell thee then base King thy Crowne was mine,
And thou a King but of my making art.
And now poore worme since thou hast taken hart,
Thou would'st hew downe that pillar unto wrack,
Which hath sustaynd Olimpus on his back.

What can he doe, that is so hard beset?
The heaven-threatning Gyants, heaven could tame,

Proud Mars is bound within an yron-net,
Alcides burnt in Nessus poysned flame,
Great loue can shake the uniuersall frame:
He that was wont to call his sword to ayde,
Tis hard with him, when he must stand to plead.

O hadst thou in thy glory thus beene slayne,
All thy delights had beene of easie rate,
But now thy fame yet never tuch'd with stayne,
Must thus be branded with thy haplesse fate,
No man is happie till his lyfes last date:
His pleasures must be of a dearer price,
Poore Adam driuen out of Paradice.

Halfe drownd in tears, she followes him: ô tears,
Elixar like, turne all to pearle you weet,
To weepe with her, the building scarce forbears,
Stones Metamorphizd tuch'd but with her feete,
And make the ayre for everlasting sweet:
Wringing her hands with pittious shreeking cries,
Thus utters shee her hard extreamities.

Edward (quoth shee) let not his blood beshed,
Each drop of it is more worth then thy Crowne,
What Region is in Europe limitted,
Where doth not shine, the Sunne of his renowne?
His sword hath set Kings up, & thrown them downe:
Thou knowst that Empires never have confind,
The large-spred bounds of his unconquer'd mind.

And if thou feed'st upon thy Fathers wrongs,
Make not revenge, to bring revenge on thee,
What torture thou inflict'st, to me belongs,
And what is due to death, is due to mee,
Imagine that his wounds fresh bleeding bee:
Forget thy birth, thy crowne, thy love, thy Mother,
And in this breast thy sword in vengeance smother.

O let my hands held up appease this stryfe,
O let these knees at which thou oft hast stood,
Now kneele to thee, to beg my lyues true lyfe,
This wombe that bare thee, breast that gave thee food,
Or let my blood yet purchase his deere blood:
O let my tears which never thing could force,
Constraynd by this, yet moue thee to remorce.

But all in vaine, still Edwards ghost appears,
And cryes revenge, revenge, unto his Sonne,

And now the voyce of wofull Kent hee hears,
And bids him followe what he had begun,
Nor will they rest till execution done:
The very sight of him he deadly hated,
Sharpens the edge, his Mothers tears rebated.

To London now a wofull prisoner led,
London where he had tryumph'd with the Queene,
He followeth now, whom many followed,
And scarce a man, who many men had beene,
Seeing with greefe who had in pompe been seene:
Those eyes which oft have at his greatnes gazed,
Now at his fall must stand as all amazed.

Oh misery, where once thou art possest,
How soone thy faynt infection alters kind,
And lyke a Cyrce turnest man to beast,
And with the body do'st transforme the mind,
That can in fetters our affections bind:
That he whose back once bare the Lyons skin,
Whipt to his taske, with Iole must spin.

Edward and March unite your angry spirits,
Become new friends of auncient Enemies,
Hee was thy death, and he thy death inherits,
How well you consort in your miseries,
And in true time tune your aduersities:
Fortune gave him, what shee to Edward gave,
Not so much as thy end but he will have.

At Westminster a Parliament decreed,
Under pretence of safetie to the Crowne,
Where to his fatall end they now proceed,
All working hard to dig this Mountayne downe,
With his owne greatnes that is over-growne:
The King, the Earle of Kent, the Spensers fall,
Upon his head with vengeance thundring all.

The death of Edward never is forgot,
The signe at Stanhope to the Enemies,
Ione of the Towers marriage to the Scot,
The Spensers coyne seaz'd to his treasuries,
Th'assuming of the wards and Lyveries:
These Articles they urge which might him greeue,
Which for his creed, he never did beleeve.

Oh dire revenge, when thou in time art rak'd
From out the ashes which preserue thee long,

And lightly from thy cinders art awak'd,
Fuell to feed on, and reviu'd with wrong,
How sonne from sparks the greatest flames are sprong:
Which doth by Nature to his top aspire,
Whose massie greatnes once kept downe his fier.

Debar'd from speech to aunswere in his case,
His judgment publique, and his sentence past,
The day of death set downe, the time, and place,
And thus the lot of all his fortune cast,
His hope so slowe, his end draw on so fast:
With pen and ynke, his drooping spirit to wake,
Now of the Queene his leave he thus doth take.

Most mighty Empresse, daine thou to peruse
These Swan-like Dirges of a dying man:
Not like those Sonnets of my youthfull Muse,
In that sweet season when our love began,
When at the Tylt thy princely glove I wan:
Whereas my thundring Courser forward set,
Made fire to flie from Herfords Burgonet.

Thys King which thus makes hast unto my death,
Madam, you know, I lou'd him as mine owne,
And when I might have grasped out his breath,
I set him easely in his Fathers throne,
And forc'd the rough stormes backe when they have blowne;
But these forgot, & all the rest forgiven,
Our thoughts must be continually on heaven.

And for the Crowne whereon so much he stands,
Came bastard William but himselfe on shore?
Or had he not our Fathers conquering hands,
Which in the field our houses Ensigne bore,
Which his proude Lyons for theyr safety wore,
Which rag'd at Hastings like that furious Lake,
From whose sterne waues our glorious name we take?

Oh had he charg'd me mounted on that horse
Whereon I march'd before the walls of Gaunt,
And with my Launce there shewd an English force,
Or vanquisht me, a valiant combattant,
Then of his conquest had he cause to vaunt;
But he whose eyes durst not behold my shield,
Perceiu'd my Chamber fitter then the field.

I have not serued Fortune like a slave,
My minde hath suted with her mightines,

I have not hid her tallent in a grave,
Nor burying of her bounty made it lesse:
My fault to God and heaven I must confesse;
He twise offends, who sinne in flattery beares,
Yet every howre he dyes, which ever feares.

I cannot quake at that which others feare,
Fortune and I have tugg'd together so;
What Fate imposeth, we perforce must beare,
And I am growne familiar with my woe,
Used so oft against the streame to row;
Yet my offence my conscience still doth grieue,
Which God (I trust) in mercy will forgive.

I am shut up in silence, nor must speake,
Nor Kingdoms lease my life, but I must die,
I cannot weepe and if my hart should breake,
Nor am I sencelesse of my misery,
My hart so full, hath made mine eyes so dry;
I neede not cherrish griefes, too fast they grow,
Woe be to him that dies of his owne woe.

I pay my life, and then the debt is payd,
With the reward, th'offence is purg'd and gone,
The stormes will calme when once the spirit is layd;
Envy doth cease, wanting to feede upon,
We have one life, and so our death is one,
Nor in the dust mine honor I inter,
Thus Caesar dyed, and thus dies Mortimer.

Live sacred Empresse, and see happie dayes,
Be ever lou'd, with me die all our hate,
Let never ages sing but of thy praise,
My blood shall pacifie the angry Fate,
And cancell thus our sorrowes long-liu'd date:
And treble ten times longer last thy fame,
Then that strong Tower thou calledst by my name.

To Nottingham this Letter brought unto her,
Which is endorsed with her glorious stile,
Shee thinks the title yet againe doth wooe her,
And with that thought her sorrowes doth beguile.
Smyling on that, thinks that on her doth smyle;
Shee kissing it, (to counteruaile her paine,)
Tuching her lip, it gives the kisse againe.

Faire workmanship, quoth she, of that faire hand,
All-moouing organ, sweet spheare-tuning kay,

The Messenger of loues sleep-charming wand,
Pully which draw'st the curtaine of the Day,
Pure Trophies, reard to guide on valurs way,
What paper-blessing Charrecters are you,
Whose lovely forme, that lovelier engine drew?

Turning the Letter, seal'd shee doth it find,
With those rich Armes borne by his glorious name,
Where-with this dreadfull euidence is sign'd:
O badge of honour, greatest marke of fame,
Brave shield, quoth she, which once frō heaven came,
Fayre robe of tryumph, loues celestiall state,
To all immortall prayses consecrate.

Going about to rip the sacred seale,
Which cleaves, least clowdes too soone should dim her eyes,
As loth it were her sorrowes to reveale,
Quoth shee, thy Maister taught thee secrecies:
The soft waxe, with her fingers tuch doth rise,
Shee asketh it, who taught thee thus to kisse?
I know, quoth she, thy Maister taught thee thys?

Opening the Letter, Empresse shee doth reed,
At which a blush from her faire cheekes arose,
And with Ambrozia still, her thoughts doth feed,
And with a seeming joy doth paint her woes,
Then to subscribed Mortimer shee goes;
March following it, ô March, great March she cryes,
Which speaking word, even seemingly replyes.

Thus hath shee ended, yet shee must begin,
Even as a fish playing with a bayted hooke,
Now shee begins to swallow sorrow in,
And Death doth shewe himselfe at every looke,
Now reads shee in her lives accounting Booke:
And findes the blood of her lost friend had payd,
The deepe expenses which shee forth had layd.

Now with an host of wofull words assayl'd,
As every letter wounded lyke a dart,
As every one would boast, which most prevayl'd,
And every one would pierce her to the hart,
Rethoricall in woe, and using Art:
Reasons of greefe, each sentence doth infer,
And evere lyne, a true remembrancer.

Greefe makes her read, yet greefe still bids her leave,
Ore-charg'd with greefe, she neither sees nor heares,

Her sorrowes doe her sences quite deceaue,
The words doe blind her eyes, the sound her eares,
And now for vescues doth she use her teares:
And when a lyne shee loosely over-past,
The drops doe tell her where shee left the last.

O now she sees, was ever such a sight?
And seeing, curs'd her sorrow-seeing eye,
And sayth, shee is deluded by the light,
Or is abus'd by the Orthography:
Or poynted false, her schollershyp to try.
Thus when we fondly sooth our owne desires,
Our best conceits doe prooue the greatest lyers.

Her trembling hand, as in a Fever shakes,
Wherwith the paper doth a little stirre,
Which shee imagins, at her sorrow quakes,
And pitties it who shee thinks pitties her:
And moning it, bids it that greefe refer;
Quoth shee, Ile raine downe showers of tears on thee,
When I am dead, weepe them againe on mee.

Quoth shee, with odors were thy body burned,
As is Th'arabian byrd against the sunne,
Againe from cynders yet thou should'st be turned,
And so thy life another age should runne,
Nature envying it so soone was done:
Amongst all byrds, one onely of that straine,
Amongst all men, one Mortimer againe.

I will preserve thy ashes in some Vrne,
Which as a relique, I will onely saue,
Which mixed with my tears as I doe mourne,
Within my stomack shall theyr buriall have,
Although deseruing a farre better grave;
Yet in that Temple shall they be preserued,
Where, as a Saint thou ever hast been serued.

Be thou trans-form'd unto some sacred tree,
Whose precious gum may cure the fainting hart,
Or to some hearbe yet turned mayst thou be,
Whose iuyce apply'd may ease the strongest smart,
Or flower, whose leaves thy vertues may impart,
Or stellified on Pegase loftie crest,
Or shyning on the Nemian Lyons brest.

I thinke the Gods could take them mortall shapes,
As all the world may by thy greatnes gather,

And loue in some of his light wanton scapes,
Committed pretty cusnage with thy father,
Or else thou wholy art celestiall rather:
Els never could it be, so great a minde,
Could seated be, in one of earthly kind.

And if, as some affirme, in every starre,
There be a world, then must some world be thine,
Else shall thy ghost invade their bounds with warre,
If such can mannage armes as be devine,
That here thou hadst no world, the fault was mine:
And gracelesse Edward kinling all this fier,
Trod in the dust of his unhappy sier.

It was not Charles that made Charles what he was,
Whereby he quickly to that greatnes grew,
Nor strooke such terror which way he did passe,
Nor our olde Grand-siers glory did renew,
But it thy valure was, which Charles well knew:
Which hath repulst his Enemies with feare,
When they but heard the name of Mortimer.

In Books and Armes consisted thy delight,
And thy discourse of Campes, and grounds of state,
No Apish fan-bearing Hermophradite,
Coch-carried midwyfe, weake, effeminate,
Quilted and ruft, which manhood ever hate:
A Care when in counsell thou didst sit,
A Hercules in executing it.

Now shee begins to curse the King her Sonne,
The Earle of March then comes unto her mind,
Then shee with blessing ends what shee begun,
And leaves the last part of the curse behind,
Then with a vowe shee her revenge doth bind:
Unto that vowe shee ads a little oth,
Thus blessing cursing, cursing blessing both.

For pen and inke shee calls her mayds without,
And Edwards dealing will in greefe discover,
But straight forgetting what shee went about,
Shee now begins to write unto her lover,
Yet interlyning Edwards threatnings over:
Then turning back to read what shee had writ,
Shee teyrs the paper, and condemnes her wit.

Thus with the pangs out of this traunce arouysed,
As water some-time wakeneth from a swound,

Comes to her selfe the agonie apeysed,
As when the blood is cold, we feele the wound,
And more, and more, sith she the cause had found,
Thus unto Edward with revenge shee goes,
And hee must beare the burthen of her woes.

I would my lap had beene some cruell Racke,
His Cradell Phalaris burning-bellyed Bull,
And Nessus shyrt beene put upon his backe,
His Blanket of some Nilus Serpents wooll,
His Dug with iuice of Acconite beene full:
The song which luld him, when to sleepe he fell,
Some Incantation or some Magique spell.

And thus King Edward since thou art my Child,
Some thing of force to thee I must bequeath,
March of my harts true love hath thee beguild,
My curse unto thy bosome doe I breath,
And heere inuoke the wretched spirits beneath:
To see all things perform'd to my intent,
Make them ore-seers of my Testament.

And thus within these mighty walls inclos'd,
Even as the Owles so hatefull of the light,
Unto repentance ever more dispos'd,
Heere spend my dayes untill my last dayes night;
And hence-forth odious unto all mens sight,
Flye every small remembrance of delight,
A penitentiall mournfull conuertite.

FINIS.

Michael Drayton – A Short Biography by Cyril Brett

Michael Drayton was born in 1563, at Hartshill, near Atherstone, in Warwickshire.

He became a page to Sir Henry Goodere, at Polesworth Hall: his own words give the best picture of his early years here. His education would seem to have been good, but ordinary; and it is very doubtful if he ever went to a university. Besides the authors mentioned in the Epistle to Henry Reynolds, he was certainly familiar with Ovid and Horace, and possibly with Catullus: while there seems no reason to doubt that he read Greek, though it is quite true that his references to Greek authors do not prove any first-hand acquaintance. He understood French, and read Rabelais and the French sonneteers, and he seems to have been acquainted with Italian. His knowledge of English literature was wide, and his judgement good: but his chief bent lay towards the history, legendary and otherwise, of his native country, and his vast stores of learning on this subject bore fruit in the Poly-Olbion.

While still at Polesworth, Drayton fell in love with his patron's younger daughter, Anne; and, though she married, in 1596, Sir Henry Raynsford of Clifford, Drayton continued his devotion to her for many years, and also became an intimate friend of her husband's, writing a sincere elegy on his death.

About February, 1591, Drayton paid a visit to London, and published his first work, the Harmony of the Church, a series of paraphrases from the Old Testament, in fourteen-syllabled verse of no particular vigour or grace. This book was immediately suppressed by order of Archbishop Whitgift, possibly because it was supposed to savour of Puritanism. The author, however, published another edition in 1610; indeed, he seems to have had a fondness for this style of work; for in 1604 he published a dull poem, Moyses in a Map of his Miracles, re-issued in 1630 as Moses his Birth and Miracles. Accompanying this piece, in 1630, were two other 'Divine poems': Noah's Floud, and David and Goliath. Noah's Floud is, in part, one of Drayton's happiest attempts at the catalogue style of bestiary; and Mr. Elton finds in it some foreshadowing of the manner of Paradise Lost. But, as a whole, Drayton's attempts in this direction deserve the oblivion into which they, in common with the similar productions of other authors, have fallen. In the dedication and preface to the Harmony of the Church are some of the few traces of Euphuism shown in Drayton's work; passages in the Heroical Epistles also occur to the mind He was always averse to affectation, literary or otherwise, and in Elegy VIII deliberately condemns Lyly's fantastic style.

Probably before Drayton went up to London, Sir Henry Goodere saw that he would stand in need of a patron more powerful than the master of Polesworth, and introduced him to the Earl and Countess of Bedford. Those who believe Drayton to have been a Pope in petty spite, identify the 'Idea' of his earlier poems with Lucy, Countess of Bedford; though they are forced to acknowledge as self-evident that the 'Idea' of his later work is Anne, Lady Raynsford. They then proceed to say that Drayton, after consistently honouring the Countess in his verse for twelve years, abruptly transferred his allegiance, not forgetting to heap foul abuse on his former patroness, out of pique at some temporary withdrawal of favour. Not only is this directly contrary to all we know and can infer of Drayton's character, but Mr. Elton has decisively disproved it by a summary of bibliographical and other evidence. Into the question it is here unnecessary to enter, and it has been mentioned only because it alone, of the many Drayton-controversies, has cast any slur on the poet's reputation.

In 1593, Drayton published Idea, the Shepherds Garland, in nine Eclogues; in 1606 he added a tenth, the best of all, to the new edition, and rearranged the order, so that the new eclogue became the ninth. In these Pastorals, while following the Shepherds Calendar in many ways, he already displays something of the sturdy independence which characterized him through life. He abandons Spenser's quasi-rustic dialect, and, while keeping to most of the pastoral conventions, such as the singing-match and threnody, he contrives to introduce something of a more natural and homely strain. He keeps the political allusions, notably in the Eclogue containing the song in praise of Beta, who is, of course, Queen Elizabeth. But an over-bold remark in the last line of that song was struck out in 1606; and the new eclogue has no political reference. He is not ashamed to allude directly to Spenser; and indeed his direct debts are limited to a few scattered phrases, as in the Ballad of Dowsabel. Almost to the end of his literary career, Drayton mentions Spenser with reverence and praise.

It is in the songs interspersed in the Eclogues that Drayton's best work at this time is to be found: already his metrical versatility is discernible; for though he doubtless remembered the many varieties of metre employed by Spenser in the Calendar, his verses already bear a stamp of their own. The long but impetuous lines, such as 'Trim up her golden tresses with Apollo's sacred tree', afford a striking contrast to the archaic romance-metre, derived from Sir Thopas and its fellows, which appears in Dowsabel, and it again to the melancholy, murmuring cadences of the lament for Elphin. It must, however, be confessed that certain of the songs in the 1593 edition were full of recondite conceits and laboured antitheses, and were rightly struck out, to be replaced by lovelier poems, in the edition of 1606. The song to Beta was printed in Englands Helicon, 1600; here, for the first time, appeared the song of Dead Love, and for the only time, Rowlands Madrigal. In these songs, Drayton offends least in grammar, always a weak point with him; in the body of the Eclogues, in the earlier Sonnets, in the Odes, occur the most extraordinary and perplexing inversions. Quite the most striking feature of the Eclogues, especially in their later form, is their bold attempt at greater realism, at a breaking-away from the conventional images and scenery.

Having paid his tribute to one poetic fashion, Drayton in 1594 fell in with the prevailing craze for sonneteering, and published Ideas Mirrour, a series of fifty-one 'amours' or sonnets, with two prefatory poems, one by Drayton and one by an unknown, signing himself Gorbo il fidele. The title of these poems Drayton possibly borrowed from the French sonneteer, de Pontoux: in their style much recollection of Sidney, Constable, and Daniel is traceable. They are ostensibly addressed to his mistress, and some of them are genuine in feeling; but many are merely imitative exercises in conceit; some, apparently, trials in metre. These amours were again printed, with the title of 'sonnets', in 1599, 1600, 1602, 1603, 1605, 1608, 1610, 1613, 1619, and 1631, during the poet's lifetime. It is needless here to discuss whether Drayton were the 'rival poet' to Shakespeare, whether these sonnets were really addressed to a man, or merely to the ideal Platonic beauty; for those who are interested in these points, I subjoin references to the sonnets which touch upon them. From the prentice-work evident in many of the Amours, it would seem that certain of them are among Drayton's earliest poems; but others show a craftsman not meanly advanced in his art. Nevertheless, with few exceptions, this first 'bundle of sonnets' consists rather of trials of skill, bubbles of the mind; most of his sonnets which strike the reader as touched or penetrated with genuine passion belong to the editions from 1599 onwards; implying that his love for Anne Goodere, if at all represented in these poems, grew with his years, for the 'love-parting' is first found in the edition of 1619. But for us the question should not be, are these sonnets genuine representations of the personal feeling of the poet? but rather, how far do they arouse or echo in us as individuals the universal passion? There are at least some of Drayton's sonnets which possess a direct, instant, and universal appeal, by reason of their simple force and straightforward ring; and not in virtue of any subtle charm of sound and rhythm, or overmastering splendour of diction or thought. Ornament vanishes, and soberness and simplicity increase, as we proceed in the editions of the sonnets. Drayton's chief attempt in the jewelled or ornamental style appeared in 1595, with the title of Endimion and Phoebe, and was, in a sense, an imitation of Marlowe's Hero and Leander. Hero and Leander is, as Swinburne says, a shrine of Parian marble, illumined from within by a clear flame of passion; while Endimion and Phoebe is rather a curiously wrought tapestry, such as that in Mortimer's Tower, woven in splendid and harmonious colours, wherein, however, the figures attain no clearness or subtlety of outline, and move in semi-conventional scenery. It is, none the less, graceful and impressive, and of a like musical fluency with other poems of its class, such as Venus and Adonis, or Salmacis and Hermaphrodius. Parts of it were re-set and spoilt in a 1606 publication of Drayton's, called The Man in the Moone.

In 1593 and 1594 Drayton also published his earliest pieces on the mediaeval theme of the 'Falls of the Illustrious'; they were Peirs Gavesson and Matilda the faire and chaste daughter of the Lord Robert Fitzwater. Here Drayton followed in the track of Boccaccio, Lydgate, and the Mirrour for Magistrates, walking in the way which Chaucer had derided in his Monkes Tale: and with only too great fidelity does Drayton adapt himself to the dullnesses of his model: fine rhetoric is not altogether wanting, and there is, of course, the consciousness that these subjects deal with the history of his beloved country, but neither these, nor Robert, Duke of Normandy (1596), nor Great Cromwell, Earl of Essex (1607 and 1609), nor the Miseries of Margaret (1627) can escape the charge of tediousness. England's Heroical Epistles were first published in 1597, and other editions, of 1598, 1599, and 1602, contain new epistles. These are Drayton's first attempt to strike out a new and original vein of English poetry: they are a series of letters, modelled on Ovid's Heroides, addressed by various pairs of lovers, famous in English history, to each other, and arranged in chronological order, from Henry II and Rosamond to Lady Jane Grey and Lord Guilford Dudley. They are, in a sense, the most important of Drayton's writings, and they have certainly been the most popular, up to the early nineteenth century. In these poems Drayton foreshadowed, and probably inspired, the smooth style of Fairfax, Waller, and Dryden. The metre, the grammar, and the thought, are all perfectly easy to follow, even though he employs many of the Ovidian 'turns' and 'clenches'. A certain attempt at realization of the different characters is observable, but the poems are fine rhetorical exercises rather than realizations of the dramatic and passionate possibilities of their themes. In 1596, Drayton, as we have seen, published the Mortimeriados, a kind of epic, with Mortimer as its hero, of the wars between King Edward II and the Barons. It was written in the seven-line stanza of Chaucer's Troilus and Cressida and Spenser's Hymns. On its republication in 1603, with the title of the Barons' Wars, the metre was changed to ottava rima, and Drayton showed, in an excellent preface, that he fully appreciated the principles and the subtleties of the metrical art. While possessing many fine passages, the Barons' Wars is somewhat dull, lacking much of the poetry of the older version; and does not escape from Drayton's own criticism of Daniel's Chronicle Poems: 'too much historian in verse, ... His rhymes were smooth, his metres well did close, But yet his manner better fitted prose'. The description of Mortimer's Tower in the sixth book recalls the ornate style of Endimion and Phoebe, while the fifth book, describing the miseries of King Edward, is the most moving and dramatic. But there is a general lifelessness and lack of movement for which these purple passages barely atone. The cause of the production of so many chronicle poems about this time has been supposed to be the desire of showing the horrors of civil war, at a time when the queen was growing old, and no successor had, as it seemed, been accepted. Also they were a kind of parallel to the Chronicle Play; and Drayton, in any case even if we grant him to have been influenced by the example of Daniel, never needed much incentive to treat a national theme.

About this time, we find Drayton writing for the stage. It seems unnecessary here to discuss whether the writing of plays is evidence of Drayton's poverty, or his versatility; but the fact remains that he had a hand in the production of about twenty. Of these, the only one which certainly survives is The first part of the true and honorable historie, of the life of Sir John Oldcastle, the good Lord Cobham, &c. It is practically impossible to distinguish Drayton's share in this curious play, and it does not, therefore, materially assist the elucidation of the question whether he had any dramatic feeling or skill. It can be safely affirmed that the dramatic instinct was nor uppermost in his mind; he was a Seneca rather than a Euripides: but to deny him all dramatic idea, as does Dr. Whitaker, is too severe. There is decided, if slender, dramatic skill and feeling in certain of the Nymphals. Drayton's persons are usually, it must be said, rather figures in a tableau, or series of tableaux; but in the second and seventh Nymphals, and occasionally in the tenth, there is real dramatic movement. Closely connected with this question is the consideration of humour, which is wrongly denied to Drayton. Humour is observable first, perhaps, in the Owle (1604); then in the Ode to his Rival (1619); and later in the Nymphidia, Shepheards Sirena, and Muses Elyzium. The second Nymphal shows us the quiet laughter, the humorous twinkle, with which Drayton writes at times. The subject is an [Greek: agôn] or contest between two shepherds for the affections of a nymph called Lirope: Lalus is a vale-bred swain, of refined and elegant manners, skilled, nevertheless, in all manly sports and exercises; Cleon, no less a master in physical prowess, was nurtured by a hind in the mountains; the contrast between their manners is admirably sustained: Cleon is rough, inclined to be rude and scoffing, totally without tact, even where his mistress is concerned. Lalus remembers her upbringing and her tastes; he makes no unnecessary or ostentatious display of wealth; his gifts are simple and charming, while Cleon's are so grotesquely unsuited to a swain, that it is tempting to suppose that Drayton was quietly satirizing Marlowe's Passionate Shepherd. Lirope listens gravely to the swains in turn, and makes demure but provoking answers, raising each to the height of hope, and then casting them both down into the depths of despair; finally she refuses both, yet without altogether killing hope. Her first answer is a good specimen of her banter and of Drayton's humour.

On the accession of James I, Drayton hastened to greet the King with a somewhat laboured song To the Maiestie of King James; but this poem was apparently considered to be premature: he cried Vivat Rex, without having said, Mortua est eheu Regina, and accordingly he suffered the penalty of his 'forward pen', and was severely neglected by King and Court. Throughout James's reign a darker and more satirical mood possesses Drayton, intruding at times even into his strenuous recreation-ground, the Poly-Olbion, and manifesting itself more directly in his satires, the Owle (1604), the Moon-Calfe (1627), the Man in the Moone (1606), and his verse-letters and elegies; while his disappointment with the times, the country, and the King, flashes out occasionally even in the Odes, and is heard in his last publication, the Muses Elizium (1630). To counterbalance the disappointment in his hopes from the King, Drayton found a new and life-long friend in Walter Aston, of Tixall, in Staffordshire; this gentleman was created Knight of the Bath by James, and made Drayton one of his esquires. By Aston's 'continual bounty' the poet was able to devote himself almost entirely to more congenial literary work; for, while Meres speaks of the Poly-Olbion in 1598, and we may easily see that Drayton had the idea of that work at least as early as 1594, yet he cannot have been able to give much time to it till now. Nevertheless, the 'declining and corrupt times' worked on Drayton's mind and grieved and darkened his soul, for we must remember that he was perfectly prosperous then and was not therefore incited to satire by bodily want or distress.

In 1604 he published the Owle, a mild satire, under the form of a moral fable of government, reminding the reader a little of the Parlement of Foules. The Man in the Moone (1606) is partly a recension of Endimion and Phoebe, but is a heterogeneous mass of weakly satire, of no particular merit. The Moon-Calfe (1627) is Drayton's most savage and misanthropic excursion into the region of Satire; in which, though occasionally nobly ironic, he is more usually coarse and blustering, in the style of Marston. In 1605 Drayton brought out his first 'collected poems', from which the Eclogues and the Owle are omitted; and in 1606 he published his Poemes Lyrick and Pastorall, Odes, Eglogs, The Man in the Moone. Of these the Eglogs are a recension of the Shepherd's Garland of 1593: we have already spoken of The Man in the Moone. The Odes are by far the most important and striking feature of the book. In the preface, Drayton professes to be following Pindar, Anacreon, and Horace, though, as he modestly implies, at a great distance. Under the title of Odes he includes a variety of subjects, and a variety of metres; ranging from an Ode to his Harp or to his Criticks, to a Ballad of Agincourt, or a poem on the Rose compared with his Mistress. In the edition of 1619 appeared several more Odes, including some of the best; while many of the others underwent careful revision, notably the Ballad. 'Sing wee the Rose,' perhaps because of its unintelligibility, and the Ode to his friend John Savage, perhaps because too closely imitated from Horace, were omitted. Drayton was not the first to use the term Ode for a lyrical poem, in English: Soothern in 1584, and Daniel in 1592 had preceded him; but he was the first to give the name popularity in England, and to lift the kind as Ronsard had lifted it in France; and till the time of Cowper no other English poet showed mastery of the short, staccato measure of the Anacreontic as distinct from the Pindaric Ode. In the Odes Drayton shows to the fullest extent his metrical versatility: he touches the Skeltonic metre, the long ten-syllabled line of the Sacrifice to Apollo; and ascends from the smooth and melodious rhythms of the New Year through the inspiring harp-tones of the Virginian Voyage to the clangour and swing of the Ballad of Agincourt. His grammar is possibly more distorted here than anywhere, but, as Mr. Elton says, 'these are the obstacles of any poet who uses measures of four or six syllables.' His tone throughout is rather that of the harp, as played, perhaps, in Polesworth Hall, than that of any other instrument; but in 1619 Drayton has taken to him the lute of Carew and his compeers. In 1619 the style is lighter, the fancy gayer, more exquisite, more recondite. Most of his few metaphysical conceits are to be found in these later Odes, as in the Heart, the Valentine, and the Crier. In the comparison of the two editions the nobler, if more strained, tone of the earlier is obvious; it is still Elizabethan, in its nobility of ideal and purpose, in its enthusiasm, in its belief and confidence in England and her men; and this even though we catch a glimpse of the Jacobean woe in the Ode to John Savage: the 1619 Odes are of a different world; their spirit is lighter, more insouciant in appearance, though perhaps studiedly so; the rhythms are more fantastic, with less of strength and firmness, though with more of grace and superficial beauty; even the very textual alterations, while usually increasing the grace and the music of the lines, remind the reader that something of the old spontaneity and freshness is gone.

In 1607 and 1609, Drayton published two editions of the last and weakest of his mediaeval poems—the Legend of Great Cromwell; and for the next few years he produced nothing new, only attending to the publication of certain reprints and new editions. During this time, however, he was working steadily at the Poly-Olbion, helped by the patronage of Aston and of Prince Henry. In 1612-13, Drayton burst upon an indifferent world with the first part of the great poem, containing eighteen songs; the title-page will give the best idea of the contents and plan of the book: 'Poly-Olbion or a Chorographicall Description of the Tracts, Riuers, Mountaines, Forests, and other Parts of this renowned Isle of Great Britaine, With intermixture of the most Remarquable Stories, Antiquities, Wonders, Rarityes, Pleasures, and Commodities of the same: Digested in a Poem by Michael Drayton, Esq. With a Table added, for direction to those occurrences of Story and Antiquities, whereunto the Course of the Volume easily leades not.' &c. On this work Drayton had been engaged for nearly the whole of his poetical career. The learning and research displayed in the poem are extraordinary, almost equalling the erudition of Selden in his Annotations to each Song. The first part was, for various reasons, a drug in the market, and Drayton found great difficulty in securing a publisher for the second part. But during the years from 1613 to 1622, he became acquainted with Drummond of Hawthornden through a common friend, Sir William Alexander of Menstry, afterwards Earl of Stirling. In 1618, Drayton starts a correspondence; and towards the end of the year mentions that he is corresponding also with Andro Hart, bookseller, of Edinburgh. The subject of his letter was probably the publication of the Second Part; which Drayton alludes to in a letter of 1619 thus: 'I have done twelve books more, that is from the eighteenth book, which was Kent, if you note it; all the East part and North to the river Tweed; but it lies by me; for the booksellers and I are in terms; they are a company of base knaves, whom I both scorn and kick at.' Finally, in 1622, Drayton got Marriott, Grismand, and Dewe, of London, to take the work, and it was published with a dedication to Prince Charles, who, after his brother's death, had given Drayton patronage. Drayton's preface to the Second Part is well worth quoting:

'To any that will read it. When I first undertook this Poem, or, as some very skilful in this kind have pleased to term it, this Herculean labour, I was by some virtuous friends persuaded, that I should receive much comfort and encouragement therein; and for these reasons; First, that it was a new, clear, way, never before gone by any; then, that it contained all the Delicacies, Delights, and Rarities of this renowned Isle, interwoven with the Histories of the Britons, Saxons, Normans, and the later English: And further that there is scarcely any of the Nobility or Gentry of this land, but that he is in some way or other by his Blood interested therein. But it hath fallen out otherwise; for instead of that comfort, which my noble friends (from the freedom of their spirits) proposed as my due, I have met with barbarous ignorance, and base detraction; such a cloud hath the Devil drawn over the world's judgment, whose opinion is in few years fallen so far below all ballatry, that the lethargy is incurable: nay, some of the

Stationers, that had the selling of the First Part of this Poem, because it went not so fast away in the sale, as some of their beastly and abominable trash, (a shame both to our language and nation) have either despitefully left out, or at least carelessly neglected the Epistles to the Readers, and so have cozened the buyers with unperfected books; which these that have undertaken the Second Part, have been forced to amend in the First, for the small number that are yet remaining in their hands. And some of our outlandish, unnatural, English, (I know not how otherwise to express them) stick not to say that there is nothing in this Island worth studying for, and take a great pride to be ignorant in any thing thereof; for these, since they delight in their folly, I wish it may be hereditary from them to their posterity, that their children may be begg'd for fools to the fifth generation, until it may be beyond the memory of man to know that there was ever other of their families: neither can this deter me from going on with Scotland, if means and time do not hinder me, to perform as much as I have promised in my First Song:

Till through the sleepy main, to Thuly I have gone,
And seen the Frozen Isles, the cold Deucalidon,
Amongst whose iron Rocks, grim Saturn yet remains
Bound in those gloomy caves with adamantine chains.

And as for those cattle whereof I spake before, Odi profanum vulgus, et arceo, of which I account them, be they never so great, and so I leave them. To my friends, and the lovers of my labours, I wish all happiness.
Michael Drayton.'

The Poly-Olbion as a whole is easy and pleasant to read; and though in some parts it savours too much of a mere catalogue, yet it has many things truly poetical. The best books are perhaps the XIII, XIV and XV, where he is on his own ground, and therefore naturally at his best. It is interesting to notice how much attention and space he devotes to Wales. He describes not only the 'wonders' but also the fauna and flora of each district; and of the two it would seem that the flowers interested him more. Though he was a keen observer of country sights and sounds (a fact sufficiently attested by the Nymphidia and the Nymphals), it is evident that his interest in most things except flowers was rather momentary or conventional than continuous and heart-felt; but of the flowers he loves to talk, whether he weaves us a garland for the Thame's wedding, or gives us the contents of a maund of simples; and his love, if somewhat homely and unimaginative, is apparent enough. But the main inspiration, as it is the main theme, of the Poly-Olbion is the glory and might and wealth, past, present, and future, of England, her possessions and her folk. Through all this glory, however, we catch the tone of Elizabethan sorrow over the 'Ruines of Time'; grief that all these mighty men and their works will perish and be forgotten, unless the poet makes them live for ever on the lips of men. Drayton's own voluminousness has defeated his purpose, and sunk his poem by its own bulk. Though it is difficult to go so far as Mr. Bullen, and say that the only thing better than a stroll in the Poly-Olbion is one in a Sussex lane, it is still harder to agree with Canon Beeching, that 'there are few beauties on the road', the beauties are many, though of a quietly rural type, and the road, if long and winding, is of good surface, while its cranks constitute much of its charm. It is doubtless, from the outside, an appalling poem in these days of epitomes and monographs, but it certainly deserves to be rescued from oblivion and read.

In 1618 Drayton contributed two Elegies to Henry FitzGeoffrey's Satyrs and Epigrames. These were on the Lady Penelope Clifton, and on 'the death of the three sonnes of the Lord Sheffield, drowned neere where Trent falleth into Humber'. Neither is remarkable save for far-fetched conceits; they were reprinted in 1610, and again, with many others, in the volume of 1627. In 1619 Drayton issued a folio collected edition of his works, and reprinted it in 1620. In 1627 followed a folio of wholly fresh matter, including the Battaile of Agincourt; the Miseries of Queene Margarite, Nimphidia, Quest of Cinthia, Shepheards Sirena, Moone-Calfe, and Elegies upon sundry occasions. The Battaile of Agincourt is a somewhat otiose expansion, with purple patches, of the Ballad; it is, nevertheless, Drayton's best lengthy piece on a historical theme. Of the Miseries of Queene Margarite and of the Moone-Calfe we have already spoken. The most notable piece in the book is the Nimphidia. This poem of the Court of Fairy has 'invention, grace, and humour', as Canon Beeching has said. It would be interesting to know exactly when it was composed and committed to paper, for it is thought that the three fairy poems in Herrick's Hesperides were written about 1626. In any case, Drayton's poem touches very little, and chiefly in the beginning, on the subject of any one of Herrick's three pieces. The style, execution, and impression left on the reader are quite different; even as they are totally unlike those of the Midsummer Night's Dream. Herrick's pieces are extraordinary combinations of the idea of 'King of Shadows', with a reality fantastically sober: the poems are steeped in moonlight. In Drayton all is clear day, or the most unromantic of nights; though everything is charming, there is no attempt at idealization, little of the higher faculty of imagination; but great realism, and much play of fancy. Herrick's verses were written by Cobweb and Moth together, Drayton's by Puck. Granting, however, the initial deficiency in subtlety of charm, the whole poem is inimitably graceful and piquant. The gay humour, the demure horror of the witchcraft, the terrible seriousness of the battle, wonderfully realize the mock-heroic gigantesque; and while there is not the minute accuracy of Gulliver in Lilliput, Drayton did not write for a sceptical or too-prying audience; quite half his readers believed more or less in fairies. In the metre of the poem Drayton again echoes that of the older romances, as he did in Dowsabel. In the Quest of Cinthia, while ostensibly we come to the real world of mortals, we are really in a non-existent land of pastoral convention, in the most pseudo-Arcadian atmosphere in which Drayton ever worked. The metre and the language are, however, charmingly managed. The Shepheards Sirena is a poem, apparently, 'where more is meant than meets the ear,' as so often in pastoral poetry; it is difficult to see exactly what is meant; but the Jacobean strain of doubt and fear is there, and the poem would seem to have been written some time earlier than 1627. The Elegies comprise a great variety of styles and themes; some are really threnodies, some verse-letters, some laments over the evil times, and one a summary of Drayton's literary opinions. He employs the couplet in his Elegies with a masterly hand, often with a deliberately rugged effect, as in his broader Marstonic satire addressed to William Browne; while the line of greater smoothness but equal strength is to be seen in the letters to Sandys and Jeffreys. He is fantastic and conceited in most of the threnodies; but, as is natural, that on his old friend, Sir Henry Raynsford, is least artificial and fullest of true feeling. The epistle to Henery Reynolds. Of Poets and Poesie shows Drayton as a sane and sagacious critic, ready to see the good, but keen to discern the weakness also; perhaps the clearest evidence of his critical skill is the way in which nearly all of his judgements on his contemporaries coincide with the received modern opinions.

In his later years Drayton enjoyed the patronage of the third Earl and Countess of Dorset; and in 1630 he published his last volume, the Muses Elizium, of which he dedicated the pastoral part to the Earl, and the three divine poems at the end to the Countess. The Muses Elizium proper consists of Ten Pastorals or Nymphals, prefaced by a Description of Elizium. The three divine poems have been mentioned before, and were Noah's Floud, Moses his Birth and Miracles, and David and Goliah. The Nymphals are the crown and summary of much of the best in Drayton's work. Here he departed from the conventional type of pastoral, even more than in the Shepherd's Garland; but to say that he sang of English rustic life would hardly be true: the sixth Nymphal, allowing for a few pardonable exaggerations by the competitors, is almost all English, if we except the names; so is the tenth with the same exception; the first and fourth might take place anywhere, but are not likely in any country; the second is more conventional; the fifth is almost, but not quite, English; the third, seventh, and ninth are avowedly classical in theme; while the eighth is a more delicate and subtle fairy poem than the Nymphidia. The fourth and tenth Nymphals are also touched with the sadder, almost satiric vein; the former inveighing against the English imitation of foreigners and love of extravagance in dress; while the tenth complains of the improvident and wasteful felling of trees in the English forests. This last Nymphal, though designedly an epilogue, is probably rather a warning than a despairing lament, even though we conceive the old satyr to be Drayton himself. As a whole the Nymphals show Drayton at his happiest and lightest in style and metre; at his moments of greatest serenity and even gaiety; an atmosphere of sunshine seems to envelope them all, though the sun sink behind a cloud in the last. His music now is that of a rippling stream, whereas in his earlier days he spoke weightier and more sonorous words, with a mouth of gold.

To estimate the poetical faculty of Drayton is a somewhat perplexing task; for, while rarely subtle, or rising to empyrean heights, he wrote in such varied styles, on such various themes, that the task, at first, seems that of criticizing many poets, not one. But through all his work runs the same eminently English spirit, the same honesty and clearness of idea, the same stolidity of purpose, and not infrequently of execution also; the same enthusiasm characterizes all his earlier, and much of his later work; the enthusiasm especially characteristic of Elizabethan England, and shown by Drayton in his passion for England and the English, in his triumphant joy in their splendid past, and his certainty of their future glory. As a poet, he lacked imagination and fine fury; he supplied their place by the airiest and clearest of fancies, by the strenuous labour of a great brain illumined by the steady flame of love for his country and for his lady. Mr. Courthope has said that he lacked loftiness and resolution of artistic purpose; without these, we ask, how could a man, not lavishly dowered with poetry in his soul, have achieved so much of it? It was his very fixity and loftiness of purpose, his English stubbornness and doggedness of resolution that enabled him to surmount so many obstacles of style and metre, of subject and thought. His two purposes, of glorifying his mistress and his friends, and of sounding England's glories past and future, while insisting on the dangers of a present decadence, never flagged or failed. All his poetry up to 1627 has this object directly or secondarily; and much after this date. Of the more abstract and universal aspects of his art he had not much conception; but he caught eagerly at the fashionable belief in the eternizing power of poetry; and had it not been that, where his patriotism was uppermost, he was deficient in humour and sense of proportion, he would have succeeded better: as it is, his more directly patriotic pieces are usually the dullest or longest of his works. He requires, like all other poets, the impulse of an absolutely personal and individual feeling, a moment of more intimate sympathy, to rouse him to his heights of song. Thus the Ballad of Agincourt is on the very theme of all patriotic themes that most attracted him; Virginian and other Voyages lay very close to his heart; and in certain sonnets to his lady lies his only imperishable work. Of sheer melody and power of song he had little, apart from his themes: he could not have sat down and written a few lark's or nightingale's notes about nothing as some of his contemporaries were able to do: he required the stimulus of a subject, and if he were really moved thereby he beat the music out. Only in one or two of the later Odes, and in the volumes of 1627 and 1630, does his music ever seem to flow from him naturally. Akin to this quality of broad and extensive workmanship, to this faculty of taking a subject and when writing, with all thought concentrated on it, rather than on the method of writing about it, is his strange lack of what are usually called 'quotations'. For this is not only due to the fact that he is little known; there are, besides, so few detached remarks or aphorisms that are separately quotable; so few examples of that curiosa felicitas of diction: lines like these,

Thy Bowe, halfe broke, is peec'd with old desire;
Her Bowe is beauty with ten thousand strings....

are rare enough. Drayton, in fact, comes as near controverting the statement Poeta nascitur, non fit, as any one in English literature: by diligent toil and earnest desire he won a place for himself in the second rank of English poets: through love he once set foot in the circle of the mightiest. Sincere he was always, simple often, sensuous rarely. His great industry, his careful study, and his great receptivity are shown in the unusual spectacle of a man who has sung well in the language of his youth, suddenly learning, in his age, the tongue spoken by the younger generation, and reproducing it with individuality and sureness of touch. It is in rhetoric, splendid or rugged, in argument, in plain statement or description, in the outline sketch of a picture, that Drayton excels; magic of atmosphere and colouring are rarely present. Stolidity is, perhaps, his besetting sin; yet it is the sign of a slow, not a dull, intellect; an intellect, like his heart, which never let slip what it had once taken to itself.

As a man Drayton would seem to have been an excellent type of the sturdy, clear-headed, but yet romantic and enthusiastic Englishman; gifted with much natural ability, sedulously increased by study; quietly humorous, self-restrained; and if temporarily soured by disappointment and the disjointed times, yet emerging at last into a greater serenity, a more unadulterated gaiety than had ever before characterized him. It is possible, but from his clear and sane balance of mind improbable, that many of his light later poems are due to deliberate self-blinding and self-deception, a walking in enchanted lands of the mind.

Of Drayton's three known portraits the earliest shows him at the age of thirty-six, and is now in the National Portrait Gallery. A look of quiet, speculative melancholy seems to pervade it; there is, as yet, no moroseness, no evidence of severe conflict with the world, no shadow of stress or of doubt. The second and best-known portrait shows us Drayton at the age of fifty, and was engraved by Hole, as a frontispiece to the poems of 1619. Here a notable change has come over the face; the mouth is hardened, and depressed at the corners through disappointment and disillusionment; the eyes are full of a pathos increased by the puzzled and perturbed uplift of the brows. Yet a stubbornness and tenacity of purpose invests the features and reminds us that Drayton is of the old and sound Elizabethan stock, 'on evil days though fallen.' Let it be remembered, that he was in 1613, when the portrait was taken, in more or less prosperous circumstances; it was the sad degeneracy, the meanness and feebleness of the generation around him, that chiefly depressed and embittered him. The final portrait, now in the Dulwich Gallery, represents the poet as a man of sixty-five; and is quite in keeping with the sunnier and calmer tone of his later poetry. It is the face of one who has not emerged unscathed from the world's conflict, but has attained to a certain calm, a measure of tranquillity, a portion of content, who has learnt the lesson that there is a soul of goodness in things evil. The Hole portrait shows him with long hair, small 'goatee' beard, and aquiline nose drawn up at the nostrils: while the National portrait shows a type of nose and beard intermediate between the Hole and the Dulwich pictures: the general contour of the face, though the forehead is broad enough, is long and oval. Drayton seems to have been tall and thin, and to have been very susceptible of cold, and therefore to have hated Winter and the North. He is said to have shared in the supper which caused Shakespeare's death; but his own verses breathe the spirit of Milton's sonnet to Cyriack Skinner, rather than that of a devotee of Bacchus.

He died in 1631, probably December 23, and was buried under the North wall of Westminster Abbey. Meres's opinion of his character during his early life is as follows: 'As Aulus Persius Flaccus is reported among al writers to be of an honest life and vpright conuersation: so Michael Drayton, quem totics honoris et amoris causa nomino, among schollers, souldiours, Poets, and all sorts of people is helde for a man of uertuous disposition, honest conversation, and well gouerned cariage; which is almost miraculous among good wits in these declining and corrupt times, when there is nothing but rogery in villanous man, and when cheating and craftines is counted the cleanest wit, and soundest wisedome.'

Fuller also, in a similar strain, says, 'He was a pious poet, his conscience having the command of his fancy, very temperate in his life, slow of speech, and inoffensive in company.'

A Chronology of Michael Drayton's Life and Works

1563	Drayton born at Hartshill, Warwickshire.
c. 1572	Drayton a page in the house of Sir Henry Goodere, at Polesworth.
c. 1574	Anne Goodere born
February, 1591	Drayton in London. Harmony of Church.
1593	Idea, the Shepherd's Garland. Legend of Peirs Gaveston.
1594	Ideas Mirrour. Matilda. Lucy Harrington becomes Countess of Bedford.
1595	Sir Henry Goodere the elder dies. Endimion and Phoebe, dedicated to Lucy Bedford.
1595-6	Anne Goodere married to Sir Henry Raynsford.
1596	Mortimeriados. Legends of Robert, Matilda, and Gaveston.
1597	England's Heroical Epistles.
1598	Drayton already at work on the Poly-Olbion.
1599	Epistles and Idea sonnets, new edition. (Date of Drayton portrait in National Portrait Gallery.)
1600	Sir John Oldcastle.
1602	New edition of Epistles and Idea.
1603	Drayton made an Esquire of the Bath, to Sir Walter Aston. To the Maiestie of King James. Barons' Wars.
1604	The Owle. A Pean Triumphall. Moyses in a Map of his Miracles.
1605	First collected edition of Poems. Another edition of Idea and Epistles.
1606	Poemes Lyrick and Pastorall. Odes. Eglogs. The Man in the Moone.
1607	Legend of Great Cromwell.
1608	Reprint of Collected Poems.
1609	Another edition of Cromwell.
1610	Reprint of Collected Poems.
1613	Reprint of Collected Poems. First Part of Poly-Olbion.
1618	Two Elegies in FitzGeoffrey's Satyrs and Epigrames.
1619	Collected Folio edition of Poems.
1620	Second edition of Elegies, and reprint of 1619 Poems.
1622	Poly-Olbion complete.
1627	Battle of Agincourt, Nymphidia, &c.
1630	Muses Elizium. Noah's Flood. Moses his Birth and Miracles. David and Goliah.
1631	Second edition of 1627 folio. Drayton dies December 23rd.
1636	Posthumous poem appeared in Annalia Dubrensia.
1637	Poems.

Michael Drayton – A Concise Bibliography

The Major Works

The Harmony of the Church (1591)
Idea, The Shepherd's Garland (1593)
Idea's Mirror (1594)
Peirs Gaveston (1593 or 1594)
Matilda (1594)
Endimion and Phoebe: Idea's Latmus (1595)
The Tragical Legend of Robert, Duke of Normandy (1596)
Mortimeriados (1596)
England's Heroicall Epistles (1597)
The First Part of the Life of Sir John Oldcastle (1600)
The Barons' Wars in the Reign of Edward II (1603)
The Owl (1604)
The Man in the Moon (1606)
The Legend of Thomas Cromwell, Earl of Essex (1607)
Poly-Olbion (1612 & 1622)
Idea (1619)
Pastorals: Containing Eclogues (1619)
Odes (1619)
The Battle of Agincourt (published 1627)
The Quest of Cynthia (published 1627)
Elegies Upon Sundry Occasions (1627)
Nymphidia, the Court of Fairy (1627)
The Shepherd's Sirena (1627)
Muses' Elysium (1630)
Moses' Birth and Miracles (1630)